This book is lovingly dedicated to
Janet McClure
who introduced us to Vywamus
and many of the spiritual teachers presented here.

Her light is still very much with us,
as our love is with her.

OTHER CHANNELED BOOKS
by DOROTHY ROEDER

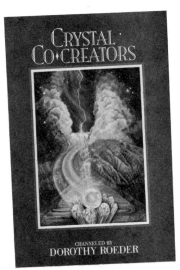

CRYSTAL CO-CREATORS

Crystals are ensouled. Those souls of the mineral kingdom want to work with you and the Earth to help you reach your full potential.

Each crystal makes its unique contribution as a teacher. From the regal amethyst to the multi-talented quartz and powerful emerald, the mineral world can open doors to experiences that change your life.

Contains newly channeled information to teach you how to become partners with your mineral guides. They can show you how to use Light for healing, enlightenment and transformation. With sixteen pages of color illustrations.

ISBN 0-929385-40-3 $14.95

THE NEXT DIMENSION IS LOVE

Ranoash through Dorothy Roeder portrays beings from another dimension, parallel to ours yet far beyond it, who give their views of what is happening on Earth now. They describe how our fear of change threatens our survival as a race and limits our ability to reach our full potential.

It is humanity's special capacity to love that is our contribution to the Cosmos.

Discover how we can help them help us and teach the rest of the universe about creating love. Explore their answers to the questions of our time — a time for healing and transformation.

ISBN 0-929385-50-0 $11.95

BOOKSTORE DISCOUNTS HONORED

REACH
FOR
US

YOUR COSMIC TEACHERS
AND FRIENDS

A CHANNELED BOOK
DR. DOROTHY ROEDER

Cover art by
Tria Schwartz

ISBN 0-929385-69-1

Published by

Light
Technology
Publishing

P.O. Box 1526 Sedona, Arizona 86339

Printed by

MISSION
POSSIBLE
Commercial
Printing

P.O. Box 1495 Sedona, Arizona 86339

CONTENTS

Part I

INTRODUCING THE PLAN

Meditation

Sit quietly and imagine that you are floating up out of your chair on a beam of light that is lifting you into my ship. The light becomes brighter but you are able to see clearly in it without straining your eyes. Everything is soft and clear. It feels nice and comfortable. You are surrounded by a pleasant warmth and there is love all around you. Your body feels light and perhaps a little tingly. You are seated in a chair that adapts to every curve of your body and supports it perfectly. Your hands rest on the arms of the chair which have crystalline ends and fit nicely into your hands. Above your head is a circlet of crystals which you can bring down around your head. There is a crystalline footrest in front of the chair which supports your feet and legs comfortably.

On one armrest is a button which you can press to bring energy into your body; this balances all your chakras and is very calming. This energy also helps balance your cells so that they can align into the ideal energy format for your perfect health. Just sit and allow this energy to flow for as long as you like. Don't try to force or direct it. Just know that it is healing, balancing and knows how to go where it is needed. When you feel that you are done, release the control button.

If you have any questions, you can ask them now. The answer will be transferred into your light and your cells. You may hear it or realize quite clearly what it is. It may, however, take a while for you to bring it into your conscious awareness. But know that the answer is there for you. Know that you can receive it consciously. It may come while you are occupied in some of your daily activities. It may come as you wake up in the morning. It might come during a future meditation session. All answers are already within you and I will help you find them as you are aware of your need to know.

Ashtar

The Plan

I come to you with great joy in my heart to be able to speak to you in this way. We are all very excited about this book and very excited about being able to make this connection with all of you. We want you all to see how much spiritual support there is for you. We want you to know, through these pages, that you are not alone and that there is much for you beyond your immediate perception of yourself as physical beings. We want to help you stretch beyond the perception of physical limitation into the expanded state in which you exist as a divine being, one who is cosmic in his or her experience.

You have all had experiences on many planets, and in many dimensions and as many different beings. Someday you will be able to remember this while you are within physical existence, and it will be part of your conscious understanding of who and what you are. Right now you are all trying to understand what you are in a spiritual sense and to integrate that spiritual side of yourself into your awareness on the physical plane. This is a beginning that you are working on now, a beginning toward the understanding of yourself as a cosmic being.

All of you have misperceptions and misunderstandings about what it means to be physical, and what it means to be a part of the Earth. Many of you feel that because you have physical bodies you are less spiritual than those cosmic beings who no longer have physical bodies. I want to assure you that we do not feel that way; you are just as spiritual and just as divine as any of us who are not living within physical existence now. You are light beings, although you have not always seen that you are light. You are spiritual beings, although you have not always recognized your spiritual roots. You are cosmic beings even though you have not been able to understand, while in physical existence, that you are.

Let's suppose that there is a spiritual part of you that knows that you are divine and recognizes that there is much more to life than simply being a part of physical existence. Let's say this spiritual part of you wants very much to be a part of physical existence, and to experience within it, to understand it and to learn how to create an ideal life within it. That is what you are all working on now as a part of your spiritual growth. You are doing your "Earth Study Phase" of learning as a cosmic being in a school called Earth. You are learning to work with physical existence and you are learning to master it. You are learning to work together to produce an environment and a world for yourselves where everyone can exist happily in love and in full knowledge of the spiritual part of themselves. This spiritual part of yourself that we are supporting is guiding and directing you through this Earth experience. It is supporting you with spiritual love. It knows your desires, and it helps you create the opportunities that you need to satisfy those desires.

Part of our purpose in being here and remaining close to the Earth is to help you discover this creative potential within yourselves that will allow you to create the perfect Earth that you are looking for. We are here to help you create your New Age. We will not do it for you. You will do it for yourselves, but we will offer whatever help and guidance we can as you do it. We are here to help you expand your understanding of yourselves and your spiritual potential. In this way we will help you to become more creative and more able to follow the Divine Plan which incorporates this perfect Earth and New Age into it.

Many of you now are attuning to specific aspects of the Plan through your meditations or through your spiritual awareness. One of you may sense the need for peace and a possible plan for achieving it. Another senses the need for more food, and for better methods of growing the food that you need to survive. You tune into the part of the Plan that contains this and you work to bring that to the Earth. Another of you, perhaps, senses the need for a particular healing technique that is available through the Plan, and you are guided to attune to that and aid in bringing that knowledge into physical existence so that it is available for humanity. All of these, and many more, are available for you through the Plan; and we, your spiritual guides and teachers, are here to help you connect into it, and to understand and create the opportunity to build these aspects of the Plan for yourselves on the Earth itself.

I am what you might call a coordinator for all of this "Aligning-into-the-Plan." I am here to make sure that each of you gets the guidance which you request and the spiritual support you need for your evolution. Sometimes this need is for actual knowledge which you can attune to through your spiritual channel or your intuition. Sometimes it is for a connection into someone who can help you clear your subconscious mind so that you can create your life more clearly. Sometimes it is a need for guidance into a particular type of activity that will be helpful for you. Each of you is moving through your own particular part of the Plan. You are always learning parts of what you will need later.

Sometimes it appears that not much is happening, or that things are moving so fast you can't keep track of what is occurring. What you are doing is gathering up the threads of your many strengths and talents, experimenting with them, perfecting them, and then moving on to something else which needs to be perfected. As you do this, you integrate each newly learned strength into the whole of your understanding. This lifetime is, for many of you, a summing up of everything that you are. When you have finished this summing up process you will be able to bring it all together and apply it all to a creative effort which is a part of the Plan. When you have gathered up all of your strengths, and when you have cleared yourself so that you can be a channel for the Plan, you will be able to create this Divine Plan more surely and more accurately on the Earth.

I am the Leader of your Space Command. We are an army. We are not an army which will create war or take over your Earth, but an army of Peacemakers and Servers of the Light. We are a "Peace Corp" which is here to serve the Plan with you and help you to bring it to completion as soon as possible. We are occasionally visible to some of you, especially those of you who have vision of the inner planes; but that is not important. What is important is for you to know that you do have much spiritual support, and that many of us here are working with you to help you achieve your purposes on the Earth.

These are not our purposes; they are your purposes. You are the ones who are in physical existence and will make the final determination of the course that the Plan for the Earth shall take. You are the ones who will choose whether to have war or peace, hunger or plenty, wealth or poverty, hierarchies or equality.

We see you moving toward a time of plenty, a time of equality, a time when each can explore his own creativity in the way that is best suited to him or her while he or she is within physical existence. This will be a time of great joy and great satisfaction for all who are a part of the Earth. That is why so many of you are here on the Earth now. You are creating a New Age which will demonstrate the perfection of your understanding of physical existence. It will be a new peak in physical creativity and will be a monument to your own abilities as spiritual creators within physical existence.

I am proud to be a part of all that you represent on the Earth, and I am proud to be able to serve you and help you in any way that I can. All of those who work with me wish to say that they are supporting you with their prayers, with their light and their love; and that they are striving, as you are, to help create the best world that you can envision now.

Exercise

Creating your new life is something like cooking. You decide what you want, choose the ingredients you think will help you create it and mix them together. The cooking process is your learning how to blend and use the recipe for living. The energy is provided by your desire to create a change in yourself and your willingness to keep working at it.

For this exercise, decide on some change or improvement you would like to make in your life. It doesn't have to be great. Work on one thing at a time. Write it down. Then list the things you need to do to accomplish it. Decide on how much effort you will probably have to put behind each ingredient. Some things will be familiar and easy. Perhaps only the way you are using them will be different. Others may be unfamiliar and will take more concentration, "heat" or will. Then you will be ready to begin to practice using this new way of directing or responding to life. You will have opportunities to use it. Your unconscious, creative mind will bring you what you want and need.

If your recipe works well, good. Give yourself credit for doing what you set out to do. If there are still a few bugs in the recipe, make a note of what did work and what you learned. At this point you can make corrections or make a whole new recipe. The important thing is that you are making a conscious effort to change and transform your life. You are recreating yourself into a more effective part of the Divine Plan.

Vywamus

"Cooking-Up" the New Age

Greetings, my friends. I come to you as a friend and an equal within the light, as one who is serving with you to bring the Earth to a new level of achievement, a new level of understanding of what creativity can bring.

I have come to bring the message from the Creator, Himself, that each of you are cocreators with Him. With Him, we can all create an Earth which will be what it was meant to be from the beginning, a place of light, a place of love and a place where each can develop their own creative abilities in the way which is most appropriate for them. The time has come to put an end to suffering, sickness, disease, aging, and hunger. The Earth can now begin to rebuild itself into that Garden of Eden which it was in the beginning.

I am one who has come to aid your planet from a spiritual or a cosmic point of view. I no longer have a physical structure but I exist as light and as a specific energy framework with a distinctly individual consciousness. However, that does not make me any less real or any less of a living being than you. All of you are essentially light and consciousness also. Mind and thought are the essence of consciousness, and this is what produces the physical framework through which we all function. Mine happens to be a little less dense and a little less structured than yours but it is a light framework nonetheless.

The key now, I believe, is to understand how to utilize your light potential and your creative consciousness to free yourself from the limitations of physical matter. Begin to see, through a focus of love, the light that is around you and the freedom that being light offers you. This is a freedom to create your life as you choose, a freedom to communicate and interact with others in an atmosphere of love and cooperation. It is an opportunity for all of us to build something of which we can be truly proud, and which we can offer to our Creator as the supreme achievement of our existence at this time.

I have been actively working with your Earth for almost five years although I began long before that to prepare for this task which I have assumed. I have studied in a Cosmic School of Psychology, which allows me to understand very deeply how the mind works and how creativity works. I have spent a great deal of time studying the creative subconscious framework, which you use on your Earth to build your lives and to create your world.

One of my specific jobs is to help you clear your subconscious minds of the misperceptions that have been built up through many, many eons of experience within various lives on many levels of consciousness. Through this clearing, your subconscious mind can begin to be a more accurate creator of what your soul is desiring to bring through to the Earth, and a clearer cocreator of what the Source Itself is desiring to make of your world at this time.

I myself have experienced 32 lifetimes at the physical level on a planet far from yours in another universe. There I mastered physical existence and learned to bend it to my creative will. I literally discovered all of the light that was available there and learned to use it. Thus I learned to be light, and earned the right to serve as light for Source, utilizing the strength and knowledge I had gained from my times spent in physical existence itself for my work here now.

It might interest you to know that I have spent lives as a soldier, as a teacher, as a mother, as a father, as a sea captain (although our planet did not have oceans as vast as yours) and then as an owner of a chain of restaurants. I really enjoyed cooking and I used to cook for my friends a great deal. I decided that I might as well begin a restaurant so that I could do it more effectively. My first restaurant was very successful. I enjoyed it immensely. I opened more and soon I had many of them all over the planet.

Cooking seems to me to be one way of serving your fellow human beings in a way that allows you to share your love and creativity with them at the same time. For surely there is nothing more nourishing to the heart and the mind, as well as the body, than food that is prepared with love and caring. I like to think that perhaps I am doing the same thing now. Although I don't have a physical kitchen to cook in, I can take the light that is coming to you now and help shape it so that you can utilize it more easily in your lives. Then you can see more clearly how to use it and how to build with it and how to create successfully with it in accordance with the Creator's Plan. There is no reason that I can see why we cannot together successfully "cook up" a much more enjoyable world for all of us to experience now.

I am not planning to come into physical existence as some of your spiritual teachers are. I think that I can serve you better from this level of light awareness, which brings through more clearly the light from a higher perspective. However, with those who allow me to experience their lives through their channel or through their openness to my energy, I am enjoying your physical existence very much. I enjoy creating with you, helping you and being there whenever you, my friends, need me.

I am experiencing now the greatest joy I can imagine as I see the light of so many of you expanding rapidly; and as I see you turning toward it with joy and recognition and a desire to move with it, serve within it and share it now. I experience great joy from the beautiful light of your Earth as she begins to shine more brightly now and to become a continually brighter light within your galaxy.

My energies surround your Earth and share with it every feeling and every thought that goes on within it. I do not reject those thoughts which are negative or not of the light. I allow them to flow past me without influencing or affecting me. I can respond to those thoughts that are light and those thoughts that particularly need more light or the help of a teacher. That need is answered by the flow of love that I bring to your planet. You can choose what to accept of that flow of love.

I am not saying that I come between you and your Creator. I am helping to focus the love of your Creator more specifically onto a particular area in which you desire to work. I see the Creator as a vast being who envelops all of creation including each one of us. I am part of the Creator just as you are but someone who understands how to use that creative power more clearly. What I choose to do now is help you understand your creative power so that you can see that this creative flow through you is what makes you a part of the Creator also.

Each of you is a creator, and each of you is creating your own life. You are using the light that you have seen within yourself, and the light that is available from your Earth, to grow in your ability to use this creative power wisely. As you learn more and more about how to use that creative power and its light, you become more and more cosmic in your awareness and closer and closer to becoming fully aware of what it truly means to be a cocreator.

So my message to you now is this. I wish to share in the creative activity on your Earth. I am here to support and help you in whatever way I can as you learn to create the life that you desire.

Meditation

Imagine that you are sitting in the center of a spiral of golden light. Imagine, if you can, that you see and feel it, maybe even hear it flowing through you into the Earth. Everything that you want and need is coming through you in this light. As the spiral flows its energy through you, whatever you need becomes a part of you, but the flow continues. There is much more than you can use now. Share this light with Earth and with everything around you. You are helping Earth to connect with this flow of infinite abundance.

Think about what you would like to add to your life right now. What would you like to contribute to Earth and your community? Imagine that what you want is coming through you now in the light. What will it look like when it is present in physical existence? How will it feel? What will it do? Allow the light to help you create an image of the manifestation of your desires.

If negative thoughts, hopelessness, fear, etc. come up, don't immerse yourself in them, but don't fight them either. Just let them pass and allow the light to sweep them away. As you release your connection into them they become part of the light that can now be used for creating something positive.

Now think of all those on Earth who share your hopes for more love, more joy, more abundance. Imagine your thoughts flowing with theirs, expanding into a spiral of light that grows and eventually includes the whole planet. As your thoughts blend there is more light available for each of you. Your creative ideas are strengthened, by your desire to serve within the Whole. The light not only feels more real. Your picture of what you want to contribute becomes more real. You can move freely in this picture and claim every part of it as yours to use and share. The only thing you must not do is hold it close in yourself. The flow must continue or it will not be there to create with you.

There are angels who help you use this light to create at the physical level, as well as at all other levels of consciousness. They are helping you build what you want to create. They will help you connect with others so you can work together from all parts of the planet. They are always available and waiting to serve the Creator through your creativity.

Your soul and your spiritual teachers are always present also to help you understand how to create what you and Earth need. They help shape your thoughts and desires if you allow it, even though you may not always be consciously aware of them. They are part of the spiral of light that brings you everything you need. As you practice using the light in this way, you will begin to understand more clearly the best ways to create with it. And you will begin to create a life that has more light in it. Take your golden spiral with you wherever you go.

Melchior

Serving within the Plan

Greetings to you, dearest ones of the light. I am one of those who is guiding the Earth from the Galactic Center in its path of light.

Let me explain to you what the Galactic Center is. There are four quadrants each consisting of three sectors. There is a governing point for each quadrant, each sector, and one for the whole galaxy. The sector that contains your Earth is being guided creatively from this particular point located within the Great Bear Constellation. This is different from the center of the galaxy itself which is located in the constellation Sagittarius. You receive input from the center of the sector and also from the Galactic Center itself.

For the purpose of understanding this within the three-dimensional consciousness we give you these locations. In reality all of the locations are superimposed upon one another, existing in the same infinite space. This Galactic Sector is a department of the Galactic Core which specifically oversees this part of your universe. It is the point from which Source's Plan is evaluated as it applies to this part of creation. I am what you would call the Chief Administrator for the Plan in this sector.

The Plan in essence is a means of assisting the evolution of those cocreator intelligences who are working within each creative framework. In other words, the purpose of the Plan is to aid in the development of those infinite potentials and divine strengths in each one of you which allow you as cocreators to take conscious charge of your life as it exists within your Earth experience.

The energies that we've channeled to your planet are designed to enable you to discover your strengths, to give you the opportunity to utilize them, and to help you expand your knowledge of what it means to be a creator. We send light which contains the ideal next step for the Earth. The essence of this light is love, Source Love which has placed you on the Earth, the love of all of us who support you in your Earth experience and the love of your own highest self. Your heart is being awakened creatively so you can use all this love more effectively as you are on Earth.

We are not imposing our will on you. We simply illuminate the

Plan for you so you can see it more clearly, attune to it and use it in developing your purposes on the Earth. The Plan then illuminates your purpose and the opportunity to carry it out. The energies we send are intended to aid you in every way possible. For eons on your Earth we have worked through your Solar Logos, and then through your Planetary Hierarchy, to bring this Plan and this light and love to you. You are now learning to see beyond your immediate Earth environment and to understand that there is much creative opportunity and creative support there.

You are learning to work with your Planetary Hierarchy, rather than under it, in order to bring this Plan to the Earth. You are reaching out now to use your own power with the help of your spiritual teachers who have served at the planetary level for so long. You are aligned with them and recognize that you can play a more direct role with them in bringing about this Plan. They have helped you evolve and understand your own divine strengths. Now you are using those strengths to reach beyond to a broader, clearer picture of the Plan, and to develop even more the creativity and understanding as your creative potential grows.

It's a process of continually stretching beyond the limits which you have set for yourselves, beyond that framework from which you have worked and become familiar. We realize that it is difficult for you to take this leap in consciousness from the Earth to a point within infinite space where you have intuitively seen your heart centered. We hope that with love we can help you bridge this gap and see that within your heart you are already at the cosmic viewing place.

There is no reason why you cannot now become a more active participant in creating your new Earth through your greater awareness of what Source's Plan for the Earth has become. The purpose of this book, as has been said before, is to help you see there is much support for you as you work to rebuild your Earth and create your ideal New Age. We want you to be aware that your Source connection is already there within your heart and that all you have to do is open your heart, recognize that it is there and use it to build your new Earth.

This new Earth is a key to the evolution of the whole Galaxy. This whole Galactic Sector has been mobilized to aid her progress in every way possible. Those of us who are working at this level are focusing more and more of our consciousness all of the time into the Earth. This not only focuses more energy there but also gives you a clearer opportunity for a connection into the center of this Galactic Sector and through that into the Galactic Core itself.

Let's say we are a department of the Galactic Core working very hard to develop this particular unit of itself which is the Earth. Until now the Earth has been isolated from direct three-dimensional communication with other worlds and other systems. This was done to allow you to develop your Earth according to your will and in your own way. This separation will be dissolved through the connections that you make beyond the third dimension, through the spiritual connections and through the trust you develop with the help that is coming from beyond. It is also dissolved through the light that you develop within yourselves that allows you to exist in a consciousness which is not centered solely within the three-dimensional material aspects of your life. As each of you opens your heart to what is within, as well as what lies beyond you, the doors of your mind will open to a greater understanding of who you are. Then you can begin to express on Earth that expanded perspective of yourselves which is aware of its cosmic connections and which is willing to work with the rest of this Galactic Sector as an equal partner rather than as an independent unit only caring for its own interests.

There is much work to be done, my friends, by you and by us. We do ours with great joy, recognizing the growing response within the Earth and humanity. We trust that you will be able to expand what has already begun and evolve it to new levels of perfection within the Plan. Our joy allows us to respond more fully to the beauty and perfection of the light and the Plan which comes from Source Itself. We hope to be able to communicate to you more and more of this joy as you learn to carry out your chosen responsibilities on the Earth in the same way.

Pain, suffering, despair, loneliness all come from not being able to see and align with the Plan. We hope this growing flow of love and light and joy between us and the Earth will help to "light up" the communicative links that allow you to see this creative movement as we do. What you need to do is release your perception of pain, loneliness, despair and grief. See beyond that and recognize the joy that is possible, the love that is flowing all around you, the beauty that is everywhere.

You can attune to me any time you wish and ask for my help. I will be happy to share my joy and my love with you, and to speak with you if you are willing and able to hear me. When you do this it would be helpful if you would open your whole chakra system. Open your feet and allow my energy to flow through you into the Earth itself. You are the clearest means of allowing my energy to come to the Earth. As you share with the Earth you are sharing with humanity, and you are then doing your part toward raising the level of love within the Earth and spreading love through your own being.

As you practice this in your meditations, it expands into your daily lives so you can learn to flow this love into every aspect. Then you will be utilizing this spiritual love we bring you in everything you do. If it doesn't always seem to work, simply accept that you have not yet allowed yourself to see it working. Give yourself time to alter your seeing mechanism. Give yourself time to learn to recognize how the Plan works and how you are a part of it. If you have a desire to bring love and light to the Earth, and you have the desire to be a part of Source's Creative Plan, you can be assured that you already are a part of it; you have a purpose within it and it has not left you behind.

Your life on Earth is an opportunity to see how the Plan works at the physical level and how you fit into it. You do not need to be limited by this physical perspective. You can expand that perspective into a Cosmic Spiritual Perspective which is there to support you in your three-dimensional consciousness. Know that we are very proud of you and of the Earth. As the creative focus of the Galactic Sector turns more and more to the Earth, know that the Plan for your New Age is already assured and that you are merely experiencing the working out of that Plan. You understand your part by bringing it about.

My love to you. May your light grow with each moment of your lives on the Earth.

Meditation

Imagine you are sitting in a pyramid of white light. Make it about ten feet on each side. The apex will be about ten feet high. It is the center of the base of another pyramid above you. There is another aspect of yourself sitting in that pyramid. There are an infinite number of similar pyramids above and below you with their apexes and bases meeting to form a long chain, but you need concentrate only on the one below, the one you are in and the two above.

There is a stream of light which began at Source level and comes through the Galactic Center. It contains the light codes for your ideal physical body and the perfectly balanced light patterns for your energy field. The pyramid is like a laboratory or factory which processes the light into energy which is expressed as matter of that level, Earth connection, physical body, emotional expression or mental concept. The codes in the light become you and your way of using light through the action within the pyramid structure.

Allow the light to flow and transform you into the ideal. You can just allow the light to flow or you can direct it into specific areas of self that need special healing or reshaping. Do this frequently, especially if you are stuck or need a lift. The angels who form the pyramids are always ready to help you. The light is their love, my love, the love of the Creator.

Melchizedek

The Structure and Purpose of Light

Greetings, my friends. I have other names, but that is the one most familiar to you. I am one of the members of the governing council of this Galactic Sector. As a part of this cocreator council, I am one of those who supports the energies of this galaxy and sustains its life through my consciousness and the substance of my thought. I am a relatively new member of this council.

When I first began working with the Earth in its beginning, I was working under the Galactic Council as a liaison between the Earth, other planets and the Galactic Center. I have learned much and evolved from this experience. I have now replaced another on the Council who has gone to a position at the universal level. I have a very intimate connection with the Earth itself, having experienced some lifetimes there, and having also worked with it very closely on the inner plane level.

Many of you know me and many of you have communicated with me although you may not recognize me by this name or completely understand all that I am. My purpose in communicating has always been to allow the Earth to experience most completely the advantages of having a connection to the center of this creative focus which is your Galactic Center.

The universe expands out of its center, then divides itself into separate units. These units, which are galaxies or sections of the galaxy, expand into further subdivisions which form the stars, the solar systems and the planets. The Galactic Center remains a creative focus from which all evolves, to which all will eventually return and which creates a link into an even greater wholeness.

My last life on your Earth was as Melchizedek, a king. I have also overshadowed other beings on the Earth. The one you are familiar with is Enoch. He allowed me to use his physical body so that I could work with Earth directly as if I were his soul and consciousness. He was a very evolved being and through his work with my energies, he ascended at the end of that lifetime. Enoch has come back to work with the Earth since that time as himself.

I have worked in the same way with (through) other beings on the

Earth, although not quite as intensely. Even now, from time to time, I temporarily come in and overshadow certain individuals to achieve specific purposes for this Galactic Center and for the Galactic Council of Twelve. I am not the only cocreator at this level who has re-energized soul aspects to come to the Earth or to go to other planets to make specific contacts within physical existence. Many of these individuals have been scientists or statesmen who have brought revolutionary ideas to the Earth. These ideas helped to move her forward and helped humanity to move forward. I am now working through a number of people on the Earth to bring you information about how to use light on the Earth and take advantage of the knowledge and the energy that is available within light itself.

There are many levels of light that you do not see. There is the visible spectrum of which you are familiar. There is the invisible spectrum which you know to be a scientific reality. There is a spectrum even beyond that which is composed of finer vibrational levels. These comprise the most subtle levels of physical matter, matter that is so fine it no longer appears physical. Your scientists have discovered that the atom is composed of different levels of energy. As you keep breaking it down, you keep finding particles of higher and higher energy potential. I tell you that if you go farther (and eventually you will) into the atomic structure of matter, beyond the physical aspects and into the spiritual aspects, you will come to Source Itself. This very center of beingness is present within every particle of matter within the universe.

The energy of this center is available to each of you as you go deeply within yourselves, peeling off the layers of misunderstanding and ignorance that prevent you from allowing it to shine out. It is not something that can be reached for and seized or something that you can order to come out. It is something you continue to search for and, finally, allow yourself to find. Light is the finest tool you have for discovering all of what is within you. Light itself consists of many, many levels of energy, from the most physical to the most spiritual. It can lock into that which is within you, illuminate it and bring it forth. What you are doing on Earth as a part of physical existence is learning to see these finer levels of light that are available to you and learning to use them creatively.

Light is crystalline in structure. Like a quartz crystal, it has regular planes and angles. Within the crystal, the molecules of the quartz itself are made up of increasingly smaller layers of these planes. The quartz understands light very well and is very good at bringing it through itself to illuminate its deepest levels. Each of you is also a crystalline structure. You can use a quartz crystal to show your subconscious how to use light and allow it into your body in a way that "lights-up" these layers of crystalline structure. The Crystal Kingdom and humanity operate well together. They support and complement each other in their use of light.

Humanity, as a crystalline structure, is learning to utilize this light creatively beyond itself and beyond its perception of its physical limitation. Meditation with a quartz crystal helps uncover new depths of light within yourselves and achieve that expanded awareness. Your Earth itself is composed of great quantities of quartz and is able to focus light in much the same way that you do. Crystals can teach humanity and Earth how to utilize light, and how to bring it within themselves to illuminate the clear crystalline structure that is there as a part of their divinity.

The Galactic Center contains the Blueprint for your Earth's evolution. Those of us who are guiding each part of this galaxy in its evolution watch carefully to see what progress is being made within each solar system and each planet. When one level is completed, or about to be completed, we send or bring the next level of evolution as light. The Earth is now receiving the blueprint for the next level which will allow her to begin to understand and build the Plan from Source as it comes through the Galactic Center. This blueprint comes to you encoded within each photon of light that reaches your planet. Each photon exists on many levels, physical, emotional, mental and spiritual, and it contains many levels of the Plan. The next step in your evolution is being emphasized within the light right now. This is the level of the Plan into which your Earth needs to move. It is being emphasized by sending you light which contains a magnification of a higher frequency of vibration than you have been able to utilize before.

This new light format is the substance you use to create and build the Plan. The light carries the blueprint and the energy required to make all of this happen. In order to utilize this, all you have to do is allow that light to flow through you and to activate your creative potential. Then allow yourselves to create as this light stimulates in you what you need to build the Plan. This light is not something which bombards you like an x-ray, disrupting your physical structure. On the contrary, it is a nurturing, supporting flow which comes from all directions. It is as if you are at the center of a focus of energy which is always there and provides everything you need.

Those of us who are consciously able to sustain the fabric of this creative enterprise, which is this Galactic Sector, form the very substance and framework of every part of it. The light of the Plan, as it flows to you, is really the energy that flows through our spiritual bodies, organized into a structure by our thoughts and yours. You are really a part of us and we are all one within the Whole. You are learning to use deeper levels of this wholeness and to expand your understanding of how you fit into it.

Light, of course, is the more obvious part of this creative substance which permeates your universe and your solar system. Supporting this light is the love of the Creator, the Source, as it flows through each one of us, your Council of Twelve. We work with your Earth and all of you, as spiritual beings who are a part of the Earth's physical plane itself. Our love is magnetic and it draws to it what it needs to express itself as creativity and as light to visualize and build the Plan.

These very cosmic viewpoints may be difficult for you to grasp but what I want very much for you to understand is that you are a part of this creative whole which is our Galactic Sector.

Each of you is a cocreator with us and a spiritual being who is a part of the whole as we are. You create the Earth as it most immediately affects you. You are each responsible for creating your own environment, for sustaining your own physical bodies and for creating your own opportunities for growth and evolution within this physical experience. As you are a part of us, you also receive support that you need from the inner planes which you don't yet fully understand. When you have grown in knowledge of yourselves as cocreators, you will be able to understand more deeply this creative process. You will be able to understand from a broader viewpoint how creativity works, and you will then be given responsibility for larger areas of experiencing in which to expand your creative expertise.

When you are in physical existence you don't always understand how much guidance and direction there is for you, and how much support there is as you learn to be cocreators on your Earth. We hope, through this book, to open you and help you appreciate, work with and be supported by the spiritual help available to you. As you become conscious of these inner planes of awareness which are supportive of your creativity, you will begin to work within them yourselves at this broader level of understanding. That is truly the level you are moving into now. It is a new level of using light of a finer and higher frequency which will help you to gain more control over your environment and allow you to create more clearly what you wish your Earth to be.

You will create for yourselves more perfect bodies that will allow you to live in greater health and happiness on your Earth. You will create for yourselves the new social and political orders which can make life on Earth more satisfying. You will learn to work with your Earth to create an environment that is supportive, productive, and pleasant for everyone. All of what you need is in the light that you receive from many levels and which supports you from the center of your galaxy.

I thank you, and humbly offer myself, and my own creativity in service to you as we manifest the Divine Plan on the Earth.

Exercise/Meditation

Imagine that you are a point of light in a large space. Make the space as large as is comfortable for you. Visualize streams of light going from you in every direction. If you do not feel you are good at visualizing, try to imagine the feeling of warm, comfortable energy flowing from you. Each stream of light energy meets other points of radiant light which respond by sending back light and energy to you. See or feel this energy surrounding you and filling you with good feelings of love, acceptance, even familiarity.

Now stop sending out the energy and imagine a barrier around yourself. This is what happens when you feel isolated and unwilling to communicate. Banish the barrier and resume being a radiant point. See how easy it is. All you have to do is want to do it. You are always surrounded by love. Just reach out for it and it will respond.

If you are in a difficult situation, reach out in this manner for light. Forget the negativity you are seeing and feeling. The love will always be there if you look for it. You will not find it if you don't look.

Lenduce

A Heart-Love Focus for the Earth

Greetings to you, my friends. I am a cocreator, a being like you, but one who has mastered creative power within every level of existence, including the physical. I have had lifetimes within physical existence in several universes including your own.

In one particular lifetime I was a teacher on a planet similar to your Pluto. This was in a constellation beyond the area of Arcturus which you don't know of as yet. In a spiritual school, I taught the unfolding process which takes you from the physical level into the next higher level in complete, full consciousness. In other words, I was teaching the ascension process. This is the lifetime that I was visualizing when this picture was given to the artist here. There were 10,000 students in my school and, at the appropriate time, they all ascended as a group. Through this process their planet moved with them to a new level. So I have had experience which I feel is helpful to the Earth now and that is why I am here.

The key to the ascension process is in the heart. It is also in the use of love throughout your whole life in every aspect of your existence. On the Earth you are learning to focus love through all of your experiences whether you realize it or not. The experiences that are being presented to the Earth now are intended to help you realize that love is the key to the New Age that you wish to create on the Earth.

Love is brought to its highest expression in life as you use your heart. Your heart is the connector that allows you to utilize love in every aspect of your life, your dealings with others and in your work with the Earth. Love is what allows you to function within your spiritual purpose on the Earth. Love is the mechanism that allows you to bring together the spiritual and the physical levels into a balanced way of life.

There will not be further progress on the Earth until it becomes possible for the majority of humanity to utilize their hearts in this positive way to bring the spiritual light into physical existence. In order to help the Earth to use love, at the time of the Harmonic Convergence, I literally placed the Earth in my heart chakra. I drew my love around the Earth and placed the center of my consciousness there so that the focus of my love would be directed into the Earth as the center of my beingness. This was not done to manipulate or direct the Earth, but simply to create an available framework of love on which the Earth, humanity and all of her kingdoms can draw as they choose.

As a cosmic being my light structure extends far beyond the physical dimensions of the Earth itself. It encompasses the whole universe. But, as I said, the center of my attention is now being directed toward the Earth. This allows me to draw in the spiritual light from many parts of the universe and bring it to the Earth through love so that you have the opportunity to utilize many ways of looking, using and extending your understanding of love. I am not the only being who is doing this now or who is giving love to the Earth in a very specific way. There are many others here like myself of greater or lesser awareness of their oneness with the whole. Each one is offering a similar contribution. I am presenting myself as an example of one who is here to serve in this way and to offer my knowledge of light to you as a means of utilizing and understanding love in your life.

My ideal and understanding of love is a viewpoint that you may learn to use little by little. As you grow into an ever-evolving understanding that love is a creative tool, you can use it to create a clearer light experience on your Earth.

I have been Vywamus' teacher for a long time. I have come to know many of you within the last few years and become your teacher also. I am willing to take as many students now as come to me. I would be willing to have you attune to me and connect with my energies at any time. I would be willing to work with you as groups or as individuals. I am not limited in the number of individuals that I can work with at one time. Imagine my energies or simply visualize a light surrounding you and filling the room. It can lift you to a new level of your understanding of your potential. You can allow my energies to help you focus the balance and the love which you are seeking within yourself, or you can simply feel my energies and know that they are there to support you. I would be happy to talk with you and help you with any problems or answer any questions that you might have.

I believe that simply focusing my energies around and within yourself for perhaps five minutes everyday would help you understand more clearly how to use your heart and how to use love in your life. You do not necessarily have to be aware of any verbal communication during this time, if you are not able to do that. Simply visualize the light and trust that I will be there.

I would like very much to serve you and the Earth in this way, and to help each one of you to learn to use light within yourselves and to balance that light through your heart. Then you can reach that perfected point of light balance that will enable you to incorporate a new level of spiritual understanding into your life and into your consciousness.

Thank you for your attention. Thank you for asking me to come as truly all of you did invoke my presence and the help of many other beings who are here now also. You did it through your desire to grow in awareness of your own light potential and to create on this beautiful planet a Golden Age of Light.

My love to you. This is Lenduce.

Part II

THE STRUCTURE OF THE PLAN

Exercise

Imagine a series of large, broad steps or ascending platforms. On each one an angel is standing. You can make the image nonspecific or you can place the appropriate archangel on each one as given in a reference for the Tree of Life or other such system. In front of this whole image, you stand with a box which represents your life. The box can represent a specific thing you are working on or simply a lack of understanding which you would like to fill.

Go to each angel and ask if it has anything for your box. If you know what it is you are receiving, good! Take it back to your box. If you don't, put it in anyway and trust that you have been given something useful to you. You will realize later what it was, in a dream or perhaps someone else will tell you in some way. Place everything in the box but don't forget to say, "Thank you." Place the box in your heart and let your heart send these gifts to whatever part of your body or light field can use it.

You are now a new person. You will be able to observe that things have changed around you slightly if you look. Try the new you for a while and then recreate yourself again with our help if you choose. We find great joy in doing this with you.

Archangel Uriel

Using the Heart Qualities within the Plan

I greet you in beauty and in light, recognizing that you are beauty and you are light.

As an angelic being, I am a part of the essence or substance of Source, part of the foundation of creation itself. Those of us who are archangels embody various levels of this light, and each of us is responsible for a particular span of vibrational frequencies which makes up the various levels of physical existence.

Metatron embodies the purest essence of Source Light which is found at the physical level. Sandalphon embodies the light of the actual physical or material plane itself. Gabriel is the astral light, the flow which nurtures and supports the physical. His plane of light surrounds and interpenetrates that of Sandalphon, forming a supportive and interpenetrative framework which gives strength to the fabric of physical existence. Raphael's light surrounds these two and forms a further supportive and integrative and interpenetrating structure. Mine is the next in line.

I am the first recognizable aspect of light which is available to the human mind. My light surrounds and penetrates that of the others and gives a comprehensive viewpoint of the Plan which allows you to see specifically how it begins to apply to physical existence. There are more levels of light. The next being, Michael, is the light of the Central Spirit which is in your hearts. He is that essence of oneness with the Creator which allows you to be connected into creation, and also allows you to be a part of this supporting structure, this framework of physical matter in which you experience and live.

The planes of light beyond that are each more glorious and beautiful, each more radiant but each more illusive, fine and difficult to understand from the physical perspective. They form an additional, supportive and interpenetrative framework of existence which is necessary for the continuing of physical existence. They are the finer aspects and interpretations of the Plan. However, they are increasingly difficult to understand from a perspective within physical existence; and perhaps it is best to leave that understanding until the others, which are closer to you, are mastered.

My job within this system of supporting light is to provide the link between the mental and spiritual aspects of the Plan and to aid you in understanding your purpose as spiritual beings. I help you understand mentally what the Plan is and how you fit into it. I help to bring the ideal which is transformed into the mental concept of the Plan that you use on the Earth. I guide and direct the Plan as it comes from Metatron and from the galactic level into your higher mind, your conceptual understanding. You can then begin to use the Plan in a way that is practical and workable within physical existence. I am explaining this to you carefully because I want you to understand there is a means for you to connect into the Plan. The Creator has provided a complete mechanism for grasping your purpose and your potentialities within this Plan for the Earth.

Once you have developed the use of your mind and the ability to think abstractly with it, you are able to connect directly into my energies and directly into the Plan as I bring it to you. You also have direct access to this Plan with other archangels through the lower mind, through the emotional body and through the physical levels. So you have many ways of connecting into the Plan, even though you have not yet explored the full potential of your divinity or understood completely all that you are in your many spiritual aspects or levels of understanding.

I am also that aspect of light which aids you in connecting directly into the essential creator within your heart. I serve this function with Gabriel and Raphael. Each one of us provides a means of connecting into the oneness that is within you and into the infinite creative ability that is a part of your oneness. We work together to help you understand the oneness within yourself from many angles, from many ways of experiencing your creativity and from many ways of using it on the physical plane.

We especially want you to understand that our light is not something unapproachable or reserved for a special few who are able to speak with us or perhaps to say they know us intimately. Each one of you knows us intimately within yourselves although you may not have actually identified that particular knowingness by name.

You have each learned to manipulate physical matter with your hands as a part of physical existence. You each know the power of emotions to create the quality of your life. You are learning now as cocreators on the Earth to expand the use of your mental abilities. You understand how to plan, analyze, and make choices in building or creating. You are learning to use this knowledge in harmony with the spirit that is within you. You are learning to express yourself through the creative force that flows through you. This comes from the center of your heart where all of your creative potentials lie and where all of your potential for understanding love and truth and beauty lie. You are learning to express these as a part of your Earth. We are here to help you incorporate these qualities into the Plan as you build it on Earth.

Love, truth and beauty have not always been understood by you as you created your physical existence. You have been learning more and more over the millennia to appreciate how much those qualities can contribute to your life. Each of you is learning to use these qualities in your own way, to create your life with them so that your life is more an expression of that truth, beauty and love which dwells within you.

The surest way you have at present to use these qualities in your life is to think about them, learn to express them and to appreciate that they are available to you. Allow yourself to see light in all that is around you and to trust that even the darkest speck of physical matter is composed of light and has great radiance within it. Allow yourself to trust that everything you see around you is a product of love, an expression of the Creator. He has allowed you to build your Earth as you wish and has given you the opportunity to create, using more and more of these qualities. Learn to feel the joy that comes pulsing through the atmosphere around you, carried to you by the beautiful light of the sun, moon and the stars and reflecting from the sparkling aspects of your physical world. Learn to recognize and enjoy beauty and truth and respect them highly. Seek to make them as much as possible a part of your life. If you use these qualities, you will begin to find them within yourself and you will begin to feel more worthy of expressing them.

All the light, love and joy that we of the Angelic Kingdom have is available to you as cocreators to use within your physical world to build as you choose. You may use as many of our qualities as you like simply by invoking them and by striving to make them more a part of your physical expression. We do not judge you if your efforts are not what you feel they should be. We do not judge you if you think you have failed, for we do not know failure. We do not know mistakes. Everything to us is created in the image of Source itself. We see only the beauty and light that you bring to the Earth.

Those of you who have gathered more of the light around you are more radiant and attract our energies more than ever before. This radiance of yours supports the rest of physical existence and allows others around you to see more clearly what is available to them. They may not always recognize it or tell you that they see it but little by little, through your example, they will learn to express these light qualities within their lives as you do. By your example you help by bringing more light, love, joy, truth, and beauty into the Earth.

The knowledge of your cocreative abilities is available to you within your hearts. I urge each of you to search within your heart to find love, light, joy, truth, beauty and to discard anything that does not fit with them there. Actually visualize throwing out anything which is not suitable for what you want to build on the Earth. Get rid of anything you have used in the past but no longer find appropriate. Now is the time to release it and replace it with more of the light that is around you waiting to come in.

There is not one within the Earth now who does not have this potential for being light, and there is not one of you who will not be supported by us if you ask us for our help. When you pray for or invoke light and love, you will never be denied. You may not allow yourself to see that you have received it but I ask you to trust that in some way you will be given that gift and that you will also be given an opportunity to use it.

You must ask for what you want. Ask for our help and then, even though you do not see that help coming in a specific way, look and see what opportunities come up for you to use it. Then trust that the help has been given to you and allow it to flow from you, for in the use of it is where you find it. You learn to understand love by expressing love and allowing yourself to see that you are a loving being who can receive and give love. You learn to appreciate light by being radiant and seeing that radiance reflected from others around you. You learn to appreciate beauty by loving it, by creating it, and by supporting others as they create what is beautiful to them. You learn to appreciate joy by using it in your life, by allowing yourself to express it, by sharing it with others and by sharing their joy with them.

When you have learned to use these qualities yourself, they will begin to be multiplied within you, and you will receive more and more of them. You will literally be overflowing with the bounty of these qualities of the heart which the Creator has given to all of you. They are your heritage as a spiritual being.

As you learn to express these qualities, you will begin to understand more clearly the building blocks for the Plan on the Earth. You will begin to see more clearly how you are to carry out your part within it. Those who are free of any restrictions which limit their ability to utilize light, love, joy, peace, truth and beauty are those who are able to see the Plan clearly and to build it most effectively on the Earth. They are able to receive the help that they need from the Earth, from humanity, and from the spiritual levels. Each one of these levels provides the help that you need in a different way. The help is unlocked through establishing the receptive, creative frame of mind within you as you seek to be a vehicle for the Plan on the Earth, and as you seek to be a vehicle for the Creator's Light within physical existence.

I thank you for your love and attention. The blessings of my light and love are yours now. I hold them out to you and ask that you receive them and use them in your life.

Exercise

Make a list of people you especially don't like or who give you the most problems. For each one make a list of words that best describes them. Then cross out the least important word until you have one word left beside each name.

Now make another list of people you especially do like or who are very helpful and supportive. Make a list of words for each of them which describes them and again eliminate all but the most apt word. Don't just think about this. Notice any emotions that come up, positive or negative, as well as any physical responses. Get all parts of yourself involved.

See if you can balance the difficult people and their word with the helpful ones and their word. See which positive words can be used to neutralize the negative ones. Which one best resolves any negative mental, emotional or physical response which arose.

Now you have the tools you need to better deal with these difficulties in your life. If you can accept that each of these people, good or bad, are aspects of your self which you are integrating, that will be very helpful. If not, simply allow the positive things in your life to heal what is not working as well at the moment. I will be glad to help if you want to call on me.

Archangel Gabriel

Connecting with the Divine Plan

Greetings, my friends. Being an archangel means that I am in an administrative position and that I am the overseer and really the composite of many other angels who have a specific task. Our specific task is to embody the Plan as it comes through the astral plane.

The astral plane is a level of awareness or an energy level which is just beyond what you can see within physical existence. It is the plane you touch into when you see a vision or feel a sudden thrill of excitement which perhaps feels like the kiss of an angel. The astral plane is a step into the clearer understanding of the concepts of truth and love as they are being brought to your Earth now. As each one of you learns to express himself in terms of love, joy, and peace, rather than with anger or fear or mistrust, you begin to learn to move in this plane. Here you can connect into those higher levels of thought and spiritual awareness where you are a part of the divine thought which is always present to guide your planet. This is available on the astral plane. This divine thought consists of a Plan which is being projected to you from the spiritual plane. As you learn to flow into this thought and connect into it, you begin to understand what this Plan is, how you are a part of it, and how you can help make it real on your Earth. The more you practice this connection and allow yourself to utilize it and bring through the thoughts you find there, the more efficient you will become as cocreators who are operating in accordance with the Plan for the Earth.

This Plan is really the embodiment of the Creator's purpose, and provides everything that you need to understand it and bring it into physical existence. This Plan not only gives the outline or blueprint for the New Age but also brings with it the opportunities to actually create it. It brings you the means of connecting into the materials and support you need to build it on the Earth. In other words, if you connect into a plan for bringing peace and you allow yourself to receive this part of the Plan fully, you will begin to achieve that. You will begin to manifest the connections with others on the Earth who are willing to work with you and you will find the support, both material and immaterial, which you need to create peace.

As the angelic energy which is forming this particular level of the Plan, I can help you make that connection. As you learn to attune to me, I can help direct you to the part of the Plan that is most appropriate for you to work with. That does not mean you have no choice as to what you do on the Earth. You do have a choice. You can choose what you wish to work with and you can choose how you bring it to Earth. When your desires and your concepts of the Plan coincide fairly well with it, a flow begins which brings you all of the spiritual support and the cosmic energy which will activate this Plan through you on the Earth. When your desires and aims are not in accordance with the Plan, you will see that they do not bear fruit. You will be given the freedom to pursue this imperfect Plan for as long as you choose; and you will even be able to generate some support from it, to the extent that you can utilize this energy of the astral plane. But by yourself you will be subject to a great deal of frustration and inability to complete what you have begun. When your purposes and desires are blended with those of others on the Earth, and on the nonphysical planes, you become part of a more powerful thought form which draws to it more of the opportunities and support to bring that Plan into reality.

As angelic beings, our part is to work at the level to which we have been assigned. We do not have the means to become physical and carry out the Creator's Plan on the plane of Earth itself. Therefore, we are very pleased to be able to work with you who are the ones who have chosen to work on the Earth to bring forth the Creator's purposes there. We offer our light and the very substance of our being for the purpose of helping you create what you want to build on your Earth. We are the substance of your loving and joyous desires. We form the connection which allows the Divine Plan to become a reality on Earth. Your New Age is a part of this Divine Plan and as each of you begins to understand it and connect with it at higher and higher spiritual levels, you become a clear channel for the Plan as it comes to the Earth.

We are pleased to be able to help you make this connection into the Plan that will allow you to understand and then to manifest a new Earth, which will allow the Creator to experience through you this more perfect expression of what physical existence can be. It will allow you to learn to understand what it means to operate in harmony with the Creator and to experience the benefits of aligning yourself with Its purposes.

Exercise

Think about something you would like to accomplish. For right now, it doesn't have to be anything big or terribly important. Learning a new technique by starting with something easy is very often a good idea. Imagine that what you want is an empty sphere sitting in front of you. Imagine there is light or energy flowing from any part of yourself that can help you accomplish it. For instance, you might feel that your left foot wants to help so send energy from it into the sphere. There may be other parts that want to help. If no part seems to be cooperating, ask specific parts to send energy into your project and trust that they will help. When you have finished, this part your sphere should be looking or feeling brighter.

Now think about or write down all the qualities about yourself that could help with this. Imagine they are energy flowing into your sphere. You can also get help from your spiritual self, angels and any spiritual teachers you can think of. If you have friends or know of other people on the physical level who might help, imagine energy flowing from your image of them (rather than from the person himself or herself). Your sphere should be quite full of potential now. Place it in your heart and thank everyone involved, including the Creator for giving you so much help.

The most important part comes now, as you move into your day. Whenever you have a chance, think about whether what you are thinking or doing is helping you with your goal. If not, is it worth continuing? If it is, send some of the energy from your sphere-full of potential, which is now in your heart, into it. If you need some direction, let the sphere expand and fill your whole aura with its light. Try to follow its direction. It may not always seem like it is leading you in the right direction but if you maintain your trust that you have a great deal of potential gathered up for this goal, everything will help in some way.

The important thing is to make conscious use of this energy potential which you have created. Just thinking of it and trusting its support will help. If you can allow its positive energy to transform your emotional state into one of trust, enthusiasm, and acceptance of your goal, you will be re-creating yourself in the image of your goal and it will become you. Recharge your sphereful of potential daily or when necessary and have fun with it. It will help you grow into a more effective creator.

Averran

The Earth's Light Potential

Greetings, loved ones. I come to you from the Galactic Center. I am one of the beings at this cosmic galactic level who oversees the evolution and progress of your planet. My particular job is to organize the light of the creation of this galaxy into the form which can utilize the Plan and bring it into creation.

I experienced life on a planet very much like yours in a universe that existed before this one. We struggled for many eons, much as you have, becoming more deeply engrossed in physical matter and more cut off from our Source connection. We were unable to see the divine light that we were. Gradually, through the aid of the light that was brought to us by our spiritual teachers and guides, we turned the tide that was moving us away from the light and began to move closer to it again. You are now at that point in your Earth evolution.

We worked long and hard. At the time it felt like a great struggle. I look back at that experience now and see the glory we finally attained, the light we finally realized within ourselves, and the enormous progress we had made in our ability to create as physical beings. I look back on that time with much joy and much fond remembrance.

I tell you this because I want you to understand that I know what you are going through now. I want you to understand that I can see where you are going, and I can see that you are not lost nor is your planet doomed. I can see much light waiting for you when you have crossed over the difficult area you are going through now.

I can see before you a great plane of light beyond the difficult path which you now tread. This beautiful wide plane has everything you need to create a more abundant life and is full of an energy which allows you to be light and to understand your own light more clearly. If you could see this, it would seem almost like a heaven to you. When you do reach this point (and I know you will) you will still find work to do. You will still find much to learn and you will still be able to grow. Your Earth will simply be an easier place to live and to express your love as there will be more joy and more light. Not only will you be able to feel this light within yourselves but to literally see light that you can not see now.

You will be much more aware of yourselves as spiritual beings, and yet you will find there is never an end to what you can learn about yourselves and your own creativity. You each have an infinite amount of creativity within you. When you learn to use it, you can create whatever you desire. When you learn to use it in cooperation with others, as you are now, you begin to bring through a plan which helps you to align even more clearly with the Creator. It helps you to see what it means to serve the Creator as you bring forth His Plan. This Plan allows you to express all of your creativity in every way that you can. It allows you to create more gloriously and abundantly as you grow within it.

If you attune to my energies, and I would appreciate it if you did so, you will find much love there. You will also find that it is a very dynamic energy because love is dynamic. Love is creative. Love moves. It seeks to expand and envelope all within it. Love creates light. Love creates upward movement, evolution, because it always seeks to discover more truth about itself. This results in an unfolding of yet more love and this love is truly unlimited. It is truly everywhere within creativity and particularly within you.

Each of you is a part of the Creator Who is love, the Essence of all the love there is in the universe. That is what creation is made of, love, which evolves into light and then moves forward to create stars, planets, and life. The purpose of this life, being the Essence of Source, is to express its love in every way that it can. Learn to do so creatively!

As an aspect of the Creator who is the Source, you are composed of Source material. The seed of your Sourceness exists within your heart itself. It is covered up now by many layers of misunderstanding of what you are and many veils which hide the light from you because you fear it might blind you if you looked at it too closely. What you do through your growth and learning on the physical plane is to understand clearly what you truly are and that you are divine. Each time you make a realization about this, some of this covering around your heart, which doesn't allow you to see the light that you are, falls away. Thus you constantly reveal more of your own light within yourself.

Your heart is the center of your being. It's the point from which all of your creativity originates. Creativity is Source expressing Itself through you. Each time you allow yourself to be creative, and to express yourself in a way that pleases you and is satisfying and productive, you are allowing Source to work through you. The more clearly you can see this light within yourself, the more of the veils you have removed. This Source creativity flows through you and allows you to express that creativity as a part of yourself and as a part of your life on the Earth.

Your physical body is not the center of all that you are. Your emotions are not the focus of all that you are. Your mind is not all that you are; it is only a limited expression of what is available as knowledge. Your heart is the center. When you use your heart as your main focus, there is much more joy, love, peace, desire to serve and move forward than you have learned to express yet. These three aspects of yourself, your body, emotions and mind, when expressed through the heart are gradually transformed into a higher and more perfect representation of what you can be as a perfect divine being.

Your soul wants to come into your life completely. It wants to work through your mind so that you can receive a continual flow of new, innovative, and productive ideas. It wants to come through your emotional structure so it can express the love, joy and peace that are available as a part of Source. It wants to come into your physical body and be a part of that so it can express itself on the physical plane, and so it can help to illuminate it with the light that is available within physical existence. It wants to be balanced within all of these structures so they can operate as a perfect vehicle for the Plan on the Earth, and so it can align with the Earth and work with her in her evolution and growth. It wants to work through your perfectly balanced four-body structure so you can be a cocreator with the Earth and with Source's Plan which we call the New Age on the Earth.

There are those of you who feel the Earth is in a hopeless situation. There are even those who bring forth messages from spiritual teachers which seem to affirm this. However, each of us has our own ideas and opinions. I am one who does not see that the Earth is hopeless. I see much potential for light. I see much movement toward that light and appreciation for using light creatively. I see the beginning of a forward movement into light, the like of which the Earth has never known. I see much potential for the Earth. I want you to know that I for one have not given up on her. I am using all of my power and light and all of my will to bring forth as much of the Plan for the New Age and to generate as much movement toward its creation as I can.

My love surrounds you. It comes on the light that you receive physically. It comes on the light that you enjoy emotionally. It comes on the light that you understand mentally. It comes through the spiritual light which sustains you on those levels of which you have no direct perception. I am only one of a group of beings here at the Galactic Center who is sending you love and light, and who is seeing this New Age for the Earth. We are seeing a time of peace and love and plenty for all. We know that it is possible and we trust that with our help, you will be able to bring it into reality.

I repeat this again because I don't want you to feel discouraged. I want you to trust in your own ability as cocreators and know that each time one of you sees more of your light and your ability to create something positive on the Earth, you create a forward movement into the light for the Earth. This light is spreading, it is growing, it is conquering what appears to be the darkness enveloping the Earth.

That darkness which really is ignorance of light and love only appears to be expanding in some areas. Truly the light from many universal points is gathering and growing and preparing to drive it away. This darkness, this inability to see light, is vanishing and each of you is helping. I want you to know that we appreciate what you do to bring forth this light which we send. We appreciate your listening to our words of encouragement and accepting our words as we tell you that you are creators, that you are divine light beings and that you are perfectly capable of creating this wonderful New Age for the Earth.

Allow yourselves to see this light and direct it against any darkness you see within yourself or within the Earth. Affirm the light that is within you. Examine yourself for places where this affirmation may not have reached. And then affirm it again. Work to bring light into your physical structure. Work to allow the light of your heart to shine throughout your whole being and then work to allow that light to flow from your heart into everything you do. This is how you learn to utilize your full creativity.

Thank you, my dear ones. Know there is much more love than you can imagine. As you allow yourselves to be light, to flow with the light, accept that light as a part of yourselves.

Meditation

Imagine there is a stream of light coming from the center of the earth which surrounds you and connects especially into your heart. As you make the connection your heart feels lighter and brighter. My love is part of this light stream as is that of all spiritual teachers working with Earth. This light can bring you everything your heart desires. When you pray or ask your Creator for anything, let this light from Earth be part or all of your answer. It supports all your creative endeavors so you can use it to activate them. It takes you wherever you want to go so move with it. It is a wonderful gift from the Creator intended to support your growing creativity.

Sanat Kumara

Your Part in Building the New Age

I, Sanat Kumara, greet you, my friends. I am also known as The Ancient of Days or The Lord of The Earth. I have many names but what I really am is a cocreator of the Earth with you. We have been working together now for eons. You have worked within physical existence and on the inner planes, as well as on the densest physical plane. I have been working from the inner planes to focus the Plan and to anchor it into the Earth with you. We've been working hard and we are beginning to see the results of our long labors.

What you and I have been building for so long is now becoming a reality for us. It is as if we had been working on a very large structure for a long time. It was built on rather difficult soil and the foundation was a long time being laid and there were some difficulties but each one was overcome. Then there was a long time in preparing the framework. Now we are putting up the walls and completing the inside and things are going much faster. We are beginning to see what the finished result will look like. I am very excited and very happy about the way things are moving now, and I am joyously looking forward to the last stages of this process of building a New Earth.

It is really an expansion of the opportunities that have always been here to explore our creative abilities and to expand our creative know-how. Each of us is an expert on one particular aspect of building this New Age on Earth and each one of us has contributed to it. There is a specific aspect of Source's Plan on which each one has been working for the Earth.

It may seem like it has taken a very long time to bring some of these aspects of the Plan into reality but when you can look at it from a more cosmic or spiritual perspective, it is a joyous experience which gets to be more and more fun as we go along. I know it has not seemed like fun for all of you at all times on the Earth but if you can allow yourselves to trust in the rightness of what you are doing and allow yourselves to see the gains you have made within yourselves and within the whole group, you will be able to see what there is to be joyous about. Then you will begin to feel as excited and satisfied as I am with the way things are going.

I wanted to bring this message to you to introduce myself as the leader of the group of all of those souls who are working with the Earth. I also wish to offer an opportunity for each of you to get acquainted with me. I know each of you very well and I know the beauty that is within your heart. I know the many strengths and talents that each of you has within you to contribute to the Plan. I would like to encourage you to let that beauty shine forth and share those talents and those strengths with the Earth as you learn to recognize more of your creative abilities through this marvelous Earth experience.

The most important tool that we have now to build this New Age is love. This is a planet of love and this is a service of love to the Source which we are performing in building this New Age. Source asked each one of us specifically if we would come to this particular experience and contribute our creativity in a way which would allow It to express Its love through the beauty of what we create here. More and more, that is what we are doing. We are learning to work together to build a structure of love and cooperation which is as powerful and effective a building force as there is anywhere in the universe.

When we allow this love of the Creator to flow through our hearts and to become a part of us that dwells within our hearts, we have the most powerful building force available. This flow of love through our hearts allows us to blend our efforts and to combine our individual contribution to the Plan for the New Age. In this way the Plan is becoming a reality. It is love which allows us to communicate, which allows us to cooperate and then finally allows us to unite all of our efforts into one purpose that simply flows from this united creative effort. Before we learned to work together so well and to love each other, there were many valuable individual efforts made and those have not been lost. They are being gathered up now and fitted into this larger structure. We are all seeing that what we have done is a part of the whole and is contributing to our purpose.

I have a crystal garden in my home on the etheric planes of the Earth. In the center of this garden is a quite large and beautiful crystal. Reflecting from within this crystal is a cross of shimmering white light. If you would like to attune to me, you might visualize this beautiful crystal and see this cross of brilliant white light into which you can merge and which will help you attune to me within your consciousness.

Crystals are powerful communicators. I use this one often to send messages to each of you through your souls. The more you are attuned to your own soul, the more easily you can receive these messages. I would like to be able to help you expand your own soul connection through your communication with me. Use your connection to me as an exercise to increase your ability to use your soul connection. Your soul is a flowing crystalline structure that fits very well into the pattern of the message that I send.

I would also like, through your attunement, to help you see more clearly your place on the Earth, your creative part within the Plan. I would like to help you understand how the Earth can support you now in your spiritual growth, as it has always supported your physical growth. I would also like to help you feel the joy and the love which the Earth has for each of you. I would like to help you experience the flowing connection that is available within the light of the Earth. This will help you to see more clearly your part in the Plan and to fulfill it and be supported by it as you serve within it. I have much to do now as a coordinator for the many energies that are coming to the Earth from the sun and from the Galactic Center. I need the help of each of you, through the attunement with your soul and through your willing participation in bringing forth this Plan.

Now you may say, "I am not aware of doing anything for any great Cosmic Plan on the Earth. It doesn't seem like I am doing much on the Earth right now." But I tell you, every time you allow yourself to share your love with another or with the Earth, every time you see more of your creative potential, every time you allow yourself to work harmoniously with another, every time you make some new discovery about yourself (even though it is a small one), you are contributing to the Plan. From your viewpoint within physical existence, things look very small and very insignificant. When you can expand all that you are, and all that you have done, into a more cosmic viewpoint, you will see that what you have accomplished on the Earth is an enormous undertaking and a very impressive one.

Please accept what I say and flow with your trusting to an easier acceptance of what is available to you on the Earth. This trust allows you to see that everything you need is available to you. That the opportunities you need to expand into a divine and unlimited being are here within physical existence. This support is available to you. The Earth is capable of supplying your need and of supporting your growth as a perfect spiritual being. Allow yourself to accept that support and all that it implies.

I am here to help you to connect with your own unlimitedness, your own divinity and your own cosmic opportunities as a part of this Earth experience. Allow me to help you to share with the Earth all the love and divine creativity that are available within you now. Allow me to share the joy and love which I receive from Source so that you can radiate this joy and love through the Plan which It has for all of you, and which It seeks to make available for use in building your New Age.

In earlier times, I was very much occupied with my duties as an administrator, but through the help of the cosmic teachers who are here on the Earth now, such as Vywamus and Lenduce, I have seen more of my own unlimited potential. I have become more able to share my understanding of the Plan and the Source's purpose for the Earth with all of you.

I honor and respect all of you as cosmic cocreators. I will do my share to help you understand the divine creative potentials which are within you now.

Thank you.

Meditation

Find your favorite meditation spot and become as calm and peaceful as you can. Imagine a point of light about six to eight inches above your head. Allow it to expand into a light pyramid. Place your crown chakra directly under it and continue with all your other chakras until they seem to be all lined up as if hanging from the pyramid on a string. Allow a stream of light to flow down through them and go into the earth so the string is anchored.

Now this pyramid is your divine connection to all higher parts of yourself and to the universe. It can be programmed to make any connection you want. For now ask it to connect you to your purest, truest, most perfect self and allow that part of yourself to fill you with perfect love, acceptance and truth. Your perfect self may have a message for you. It may just want to be part of you and be available to you as a connection.

Now you can use the connection you are building to ask a question or to seek out a specific spiritual entity for communication. Make your request and step out of the way with your own thoughts. Try to make your mind into a clear, reflecting pool which will respond without interference to any thoughts that come. If you get pictures, ask for the meaning behind the images. If you get thoughts in the form of words, just let them flow. Evaluate them later. Judging them now may interfere with the connection.

If you get something that feels wrong, let it go, recenter and reactivate your pyramid. Do not judge yourself in any way. Everything that comes is light and potentially positive when you have learned to use it. Looking at it from many viewpoints allows you to find the best way to use all available light. Don't focus on what is difficult. Ask your pyramid to bring you the highest and best that you are so that it will become part of you. Each time you use it, your connection becomes stronger.

Archangel Metatron

Your Source Connection

Greetings, dear ones. I am the archangel who embodies the highest level of physical existence. This includes what is unknown and unseen at your present conscious level of perception. My energies pervade all of physical existence and serve as what you might call your highest connection into Source. I am a bridge that connects Source and the Creator directly into physical existence. All of you are creators with the Source. You are learning to recognize all of your creative abilities. I can help you to connect into that highest part of yourself which is the clearest aspect of the Source connection or your Source Beingness.

We of the Angelic Kingdom do not create consciously as humans do. We simply are extensions of Source and we are the Source substance with which you create. Therefore, as creators, you are the ones who direct the use of our energies and you are the ones who decide what we will create within physical existence. We embody Source's Plan Itself. When you choose to work with this Plan and to utilize It, it is our energies which form your connection into It. Without your decision to utilize what we are and to become a part of this Plan, we remain simply a blueprint or an energy flow which does not connect into anything specific. Without your conscious desire to use our spiritual energies, we remain simply undifferentiated Source substance which has not had the opportunity to become a part of physical existence; our energies are not able to connect into the potentials that are there within physical existence, and they can not help it to bloom, grow and express all that the Creator has chosen to express through it. Without you we cannot participate in the development of your creative opportunities which Source has given you on Earth.

You might look at us as a flow which allows Source to be present within physical existence and to be expressed as physical substance on your Earth. All that you see around you as physical matter is Source substance which has been converted into physical matter through your conscious desire to create.

There are ten archangels who serve as ten levels of the Plan for your Earth. I am the one that is most like the energy of Source. There are others who embody the other planes of physical existence. Each one of us has specific aspects of ourselves that operate at our energy level, working within other angelic beings who make up the totality of all that we are. They are also here to serve the purpose and the desires of the Creator and of you as cocreators.

Source has chosen to become physical through each of you. You serve as cocreators with Source to build your Earth and to give it an increasingly more spiritual expression. The level you are working on at this time is called the New Age.

The archangels embody the skeletal structure of the Plan which Source has for the Earth and for the New Age. Each angelic energy is a stepping stone to the next higher level of understanding the Source Plan. Each step is necessary for the continuity of its flow into physical existence and none is more important than any other. It is not necessary for you to understand completely each of these creative levels of the Plan but it is necessary for you to understand clearly what you are building and what you desire to create on your Earth. The higher you are able to stretch in your consciousness, the more clearly you can see the whole picture and the more easily you can see how your part fits into the whole and how all of the cocreators serve the Plan as a complete unit.

Many of you now are beginning to see your purposes in terms of the whole, and are beginning to realize the importance of working together as a group to bring forth the New Age. The time for individual efforts has passed. The efforts which have meaning now and are effective will be those that take into account the abilities, desires and purposes of a group. We can help you blend the energies of your group at whatever level that group can reach. We can help you to gain an even greater understanding of how these work together. Some groups may work with a few levels of the Divine Plan and a few levels of archangelic energies. Others, through their clarity of vision and their ability to connect into higher aspects of the Plan, use more of these levels of angelic energies. Each group receives the help it needs and which it is capable of using. As the group grows and matures, it is able to handle greater amounts and finer aspects of angelic energy. Then it is able to enter deeper and higher levels of the Plan itself.

Those of you who choose to make an effort to communicate with me will receive whatever help you need to connect into the appropriate level at which you are working as a creator. I will help you connect into the Plan and realize your purpose. I will aid you in making the most of your opportunities on the Earth. I am working to help you connect into the Plan at the galactic level.

My energies are bringing to the Earth the Divine Blueprint which you need to create a more efficient creative structure from your own physical bodies. This light which I am, and which I focus from the

Galactic Center, carries the next level of the Divine Blueprint which you need to pattern your physical structure for existence in the New Age. As you desire to serve the Plan and allow yourselves to become a part of it, you become connected into these higher energies. This energy of the Plan is being used within your physical structure to make your body stronger, more efficient, and closer to the ideal. You will be able to create for yourselves bodies which never get sick, which do not age, and which will serve you by becoming exactly what you want them to be.

If your purposes and desires are in line with the Plan, this creative opportunity for building a perfect physical structure comes much more easily. The design of this new structure allows an easier connection into your own Source level awareness and a clearer connection to your Creator. Those who do not desire to align with the Plan are clearly not able to utilize this Divine Blueprint. It will not suit their purposes as they selfishly seek something which is not a part of the Plan.

There are many angelic beings who help me provide this connection into Source's Plan for you. There are many spiritual teachers who are available now to help you allow this connection and help you understand more fully how to use it. I am one who is here to serve you as you create your New Age on Earth. I am one who humbly offers his services to all of you as cocreators of your New Earth. I have worked with many of you before at different levels of your understanding and at different levels of beingness. I am available now to continue that relationship and to serve you as creators in any way that I can.

Thank you.

Exercise

Open a link with me through whatever meditative method seems easiest to you. You can use the technique given by Metatron in the last chapter. My energy may be hard to detect by any sense or awareness because I am coming through a very deep, natural part of yourself. You will perhaps feel only a shift in your own energy that makes you feel more secure and confident with yourself. Just allow the connection for a few moments without judging whether you are doing it correctly or getting the right things.

I am going to give you a list of strengths I see in you. I ask you to write them down whether you believe them or not. Trusting what comes through your channel is part of developing it. And I can see more of you than you can. I can see a great deal of what you are becoming. Your list may be short or long for now. I may have much more later but want you to focus on one thing at a time.

Take one item from your list and move with it physically somehow. Pretend that you really are the quality or strength and take it for a walk, trying to feel what it is like to really have it and express it. How does it influence how you interact with others? I will help you if you do your best to maintain your connection with me. Some other time, during some other activity, try it again or try the next item on your list. Together we will build on your strengths and your ability to use them creatively.

Atlanto

Becoming a Part of the Whole

Greetings. I am delighted at this opportunity to make myself and my purposes known to you. I will try to explain something of what I am although it will be difficult for you to understand all of what that means at the physical level.

I am one of the twelve beings who focus the energy or the thought which is sustaining this cosmic day's experience. This thought is the framework which is creating this universal experience. This thought comes from Source Itself and is transposed through our integrated understanding into the purpose and the substance of this experience. All that you see and feel around you is simply the energy of thought. Each of you experiences a life which you, yourselves, have projected through your thoughts, both consciously and subconsciously, which are then the framework of the universal experience. Your life is evolving along the lines of opportunity which are presented by the thoughts of those of us who have focused this experience, this opportunity.

When I say there are twelve beings who are focusing the thought of this cosmic day, I am including eleven of us who remain aware in our full cosmic consciousness. The twelfth one consists of all of those others who are taking part in this cosmic experience, all of those who are cocreators and who are learning to be cocreators. They all work in harmony with the 11 others to focus the will of Divine Source Itself. You do not now feel like one great being but you are learning to do so. You learn first by loving. You blend your creative desires with your own loved ones, individually or as a group. Then you learn to expand your ability to interact creatively with others into larger and larger groups.

As these lessons are learned, you will find more and more that you do not have a will of your own. You do not have an individual consciousness. You are a part of a larger consciousness that has a purpose, one that is evolving and growing into a clearer understanding of itself, and one that is evolving and growing into a clearer ability to carry through the purposes of Source for this cosmic day. Each one of you has been given a sacred mission to be a part of this creative experience and to cooperate with others in a way that allows this experience to come to its intended conclusion.

Many of you have sensed a spiritual purpose for yourself. This is good. You act on that and move in the direction of fulfilling that purpose. Many times you look at it very personally, without understanding how it fits into the whole creative movement. Source has divided this experience into separate aspects. Each of you has assumed conscious responsibility for one of these aspects. Each aspect is a part of the whole which contains the wholeness within it and yet serves to fulfill a particular function within the whole. The understanding of the whole can evolve and eventually be yours but you are not expected to do it all yourself. You will eventually be able to utilize the learning and the growth of others as a part of your own growth, sharing in what others accomplish and utilizing that framework as a part of your own.

This sharing is done through the use of the heart, using an energy connection which is made there. It allows you to feel a part of the whole, to learn to use the energies of the whole and to contribute your part to the whole, not seeking anything for yourself but seeking only to serve the whole. Those of us who serve as the cocreators of this universe do so with a complete awareness of the contribution of each, a complete sharing of our energies, a complete sharing of the understanding of each, and a respect for the contribution of each individual within this whole universal experience.

I had experiences within the physical many cosmic days ago. I grew and learned through those experiences to understand my own unlimitedness until now I have become able to focus the wholeness of creation and feel a part of it. I can now share every aspect of that creative opportunity. I am aware of all that is going on but I do not do it all. I have not created everything. What I cannot do, or what is not appropriate for me to do, I allow another to do so as to complete what is needed. There is no thought of self gain or selfish purpose. We see only the good of the whole and its forward movement.

After you have understood physical existence as completely as you choose to at this time, you will move on to other, more cosmic experiences where you take on more responsibility and a greater share of the "load" (although it is not really a load) in focusing the thought or the energy of a creative experience. Each gain in awareness leads to a clearer understanding of the whole and a clearer ability to be able to focus the will and the purpose of the whole.

I am not directly involved in focusing the specific purposes of your New Age on the Earth right now. My purposes are rather more cosmic. There are those at other levels of understanding who take the energy of the thought which is projected from this level, and interpret it and step it down to the succeeding levels until it finally reaches your Earth's Hierarchy and your human consciousness. It is not really possible for me to focus the purposes as understood at this level into a meaningful statement which can be accepted within physical existence. It was not intended that I should. This offers an opportunity to those many other beings to bring this purpose to you. It is an opportunity for them to grow and evolve in their ability to focus this great Cosmic Plan.

My purpose in coming is to allow you a closer connection with that which dwells within you, that core of your heart which is Source. You can connect specifically with my energy if you choose. I will be happy to talk to you or to focus my energy for you. I am not limited in any way in my ability to do this. I will not tell you what to do in your day-to-day life; I cannot answer your questions as to how you can solve a specific problem or what your choices should be in moving forward now. I can, however, focus for you an understanding of where you are going and help you move a little closer to it and to your understanding of how your purpose fits into the whole.

If you ask me for help, I will always hear you and the help will be given. It may not be given exactly the way you thought it would be because I perhaps see things differently than you. But you can trust that the love and the light that I send will, in some way, apply to the problem you are having, and it will help you to move closer to the solution of it.

My message to you is now a simple one. I am not going to try to explain to you a vast complicated scheme of how the universe is designed and how you fit into it. That will perhaps come later. The purpose now is to simply let you know that I am here to serve as an anchor for you into that Sourceness of which you are a part and which dwells within you. I am here to help you uncover that Sourceness and begin to utilize It in your lives by discovering your strengths, and by using all of those gifts which Source has given to you specifically to further Its Plan.

My love for you is great. I don't think you can understand how much we all do love you, how much we trust you, and how joyous we feel at every step that you take, as every realization that you make brings you closer and closer to an understanding of what you truly are. What I am, all of you can one day become. I hope that by focusing my energy more specifically into this beautiful planet, it will help all of you to better understand and utilize the creative opportunity that you have here on your Earth.

I do not bring my energies directly to you; they would be too overwhelming for you. I focus my energies through two lakes on the Earth, one in Kansas and one in Tibet. I also focus them through your own soul structure if you are able to use it. I would like you to look at a relationship with me as simply another way of understanding how you fit into the whole and how you can interact with it as a divine creative being.

I would like to serve as another loving friend and guide who is here to help you along your way, to send you some of the energies which will help you build your new Earth, and to create the life of peace and joy and light which you are seeking. I do not bring any kind of judgment, any kind of punishment, any kind of decision about what you should do or how you should run your life or your Earth. I am simply here to focus love, love as the foundation of the Plan which Source is evolving throughout this whole universal experience.

I am hoping to aid you in understanding that love will connect you into your part in this Plan. It will help you unfold your strengths and will guide you into becoming a functioning part of the whole. Love will allow you to interact within the whole in the most appropriate way. You each have specific talents which have been given to you to use in this creative effort and you each have the opportunities to use them. Everything you have can be used by Source, and everything you have will become a part of the forward movement of the whole. I hope to help you to understand that aligning with this group process on Earth is truly the most spiritual and the most satisfying thing that you can do.

I ask that you not be intimidated by what I am as you make your approach to me but simply understand that I look upon each one of you as equally important within this creation and equally deserving of all of the love that I can bring. I know that I will have the opportunity to share my love with you in whatever way you choose to allow it.

Thank you for this opportunity to speak with you and tell you of my desires. I ask you to continue to grow and to continue to share your strengths with the Whole so that we can all move together to a most glorious conclusion for this cosmic day. When that glorious conclusion comes about, we will all be together in every way. We will be able to share completely all that we are with the Whole. Thank you.

Exercise/Mediation

Find a place where you can feel peaceful and quiet. Imagine or know that you are surrounded by a large bubble, full of iridescent white light. Allow yourself to enjoy the light for a few moments, see sparks swirling around you or feel it as pleasantly warm and slightly tingling. If you move to another place your light goes with you.

Know that this light is your soul and its love for you. Invite your soul to be present with you within the light. Ask your soul a question about anything you want to understand or any problem you have. Then imagine you are your soul thinking and feeling about the question. What thoughts come into your mind? Some may be old familiar thoughts. Those are okay, but let them go. Just focus on experiencing as many as you can. Some of them could be new and quite exciting as you gradually learn to see things from a new perspective.

As you practice this soul perspective, you will be able to do it in many different places and circumstances. Remember to act on any positive suggestions you receive so you will make the new viewpoint part of your life flow.

El Morya

Surrendering to the Plan

Welcome, my friends, to the doorway of the New Age. That is where we are standing now and that is the point from which we are seeking to move and to choose our direction. We are in the doorway of a great opportunity to move forward in our understanding of how to use love and how to work with light on this Earth in a very creative way that has never been accomplished before. We have a Divine Plan which is available to guide us in this process.

I am called the Master El Morya. I am a part of the First Ray Department or the department that is concerned with establishing the Divine Will for the Earth. I work very closely with the Master Kuthumi and we have been friends for a very long time. I was one of the Three Wise Men. I have also spent many, many lifetimes in India; as a prince, as a holy man, as a business leader, to give a few. I will not give you names here because they are not part of the common knowledge in your history and wouldn't have much meaning for you. I also spent some lifetimes in the West; in America about 5000 years ago, in South America as an Inca Indian and also as an Aztec High Priest. I had some very rewarding experiences in Atlantis with many of you as we built the light into a creative vehicle there which left many of the seeds we are now utilizing to build the New Age. I was a pharaoh in Egypt but that was before your recorded history.

My work now involves bringing to Earth the Will of Sanat Kumara, the Lord of the Earth, as he seeks to interpret and bring forth this new Plan for the Earth. It requires some interpretation on my part also because I am an individual (as all of you are) with a unique pattern of consciousness that works in its own way. But I try to remain open to how my interpretation affects and blends in with that of others.

There is always much communication here within the Hierarchy. We are all always seeking to adapt our interpretation of the Plan to that of the whole and to that of the leaders of the Hierarchy, particularly the Christ and Sanat Kumara. In this way, we would like to aid you in developing this ability to attune to the Divine Plan and to utilize your viewpoint in the most effective way at the physical level on the Earth.

I recognize that all of you are working also at the spiritual level.

At that level, your soul understands the Plan much more clearly than you do on the physical level. Your physical plane viewpoint is a unique and very useful one. It is the one that is the most closely attuned to, and associated with, the actual needs of the physical plane. No decisions are ever made from this Hierarchical level without taking into account the feelings of those on the Earth and their ability to utilize any changes or emphasis that we might seek to bring through to you. So you see we are not only attuning to each other here within the Hierarchy but to you also, as working partners with us. Each of you has your own purposes for your physical life. Each of you has your own needs and your own desires. And each of you has a unique viewpoint which is important to us and to the Whole.

Some of you are already learning to listen to your soul's guidance in these matters. All of you are seeking to become more closely guided by your soul. Sometimes it seems, as you reach a point where you must surrender to the will of the soul, that you are going to lose a vital part of yourself, that something will be taken away from you, and that perhaps you will have to give up something that's very important. There are many misperceptions that as you tread a spiritual path you have to give up everything that is material. This is not always true. What you have to give up is the feeling that material things are the most important. You need to achieve a balance in your use of material things that allows the spiritual side of yourself to make use of them in the most effective way possible. There is a great need now, for instance, for people working within the Plan who can attract money as a spiritual resource and use it effectively for the benefit of the Whole.

Another thing that appears to be lost as you surrender to the soul is the feeling of importance that you have as an individual. It seems that as your soul takes over, your individual importance begins to diminish rapidly. Sometimes a fear pattern sets in which causes you to pull away from the soul. Again, what needs to be balanced is your own uniqueness with the needs of the whole. We have no need of individuals who wish to express their individuality in ways that harm others or take away from others. What we do need are individuals who are aware of their unique strengths and who are willing to offer them freely and joyously to the efforts of the whole. We need individuals who are willing to make a contribution in the way that they are most able to do so.

Even love can seem to be confusing as you approach a point of surrender to the soul. It seems sometimes that perhaps you must give up everything that you love in order to allow the soul to be a part of your life. Here again, it is not giving up what you love at the physical level but gaining a whole new world of understanding of what love is at a more cosmic level. We have no need now for individuals who give up their friends and family and go off in search of some grand spiritual opportunity. What we need are people who can expand the love they have for their friends and their family into a love for all of humanity, a love that is not separative, a love that is willing to share with all who are willing to receive, a love that does not feel superior to anyone else, a love that is simply there and radiant and that is constantly moving and flowing with the pattern of the Plan.

So when you surrender to the soul or the Divine Will, what you are really doing is gaining a whole new world of experience, a whole new viewpoint that allows you to see a much grander picture of the opportunities that are here now as a part of the Earth. This is a viewpoint which allows you to suddenly see that the Earth is here to help you and support you. It was not intended to provide the experience of suffering, pain, loss and separation from the divine parts of yourself. The Earth is a very loving being, a very supportive being. She is learning how to use these qualities just as you are and how to share them with each aspect of herself. As you learn to share your love and your support with humanity and with the animals, the plants, the Mineral Kingdom — as you learn to share your responsibility with the Earth — you aid her in growing in her own ability to align into the Divine Plan and to surrender to It.

It takes great love in order to align with the Plan but it also takes an effort of will. It takes great determination to see a pathway and to stick to it until you have managed to release all of the blocks and objections within self that tend to make you want to wander away from it. It takes great determination to say, "I know that I am a divine being and I refuse to surrender to the idea that I am simply a physical body, a collection of atoms which has no relationship to anything divine." It also takes a great deal of will to allow yourself to release what is no longer needed, even after you have seen how little you need it. It's not easy to say, "I refuse to feel inferior any longer, even though others seem to reflect back to me that they do not accept that I have a valid offering to make here." It takes courage to keep trusting in divine guidance when old habit patterns keep leading you into areas where there does not seem to be any guidance.

It takes great determination to say, "I know I am divine. I know there is a place for me within the Plan. I am willing to look within myself to uncover these strengths that I have, and to use them now for the whole without any reservations and without any restrictions." It takes great trust to open one's self to the energies of the soul which seem unfamiliar and inappropriate to the physical body. But know that when you invoke the help of your soul, and when you invoke the help of the spiritual teachers, that guidance will be given in the most appropriate way. Your life can begin to change its direction so that little by little you can see more clearly that you are making the progress you wish.

More and more, the whole Earth is beginning to see now that progress is being made. There is a coming together of the separate energies of humanity into a magnetic, centered, directional movement that is pulling everything into it, into alignment with this Plan which is becoming more and more a part of what is going on in the Earth now. Let's say that the Plan is being anchored into the Earth through your desire to bring it forth. As more people can understand it, and begin to work with it, the stronger and more magnetic it gets. The more people are drawn into it, the easier it is to see and use. All of those activities and ideas on the Earth which are not a part of it will simply fade away from disuse.

I would say now to have heart, my friends. You are all doing very well. The Plan is moving forward at a rate that it has never moved before. It is being accepted in more ways than it has ever been accepted before. We see much light growing on the Earth as a result of it, and much greater potential for it to receive our help and to allow us to work with you. The more the Plan becomes a part of the Earth's forward movement, the closer we are able to come to the Earth to be with you, to guide you and to share with you the fruits of this labor which is the building of the New Age.

When the Plan is firmly anchored into the Earth and is functioning at somewhere close to 50%, you will see many of us, your spiritual teachers, appearing on the Earth. We will become a part of the actual movement of physical existence that you are creating. This has been promised and it will occur. Be strong in the knowledge that each of you has the strength that you need to carry out your part in the New Age and to help to bring it about.

Trust and know that you are receiving all the help from us on the spiritual plane that we can bring to you. Our purpose here is to help the Earth to evolve and to grow and to see each one of you learn to use your creative powers more effectively and more in alignment with the Plan. As we do this, we grow in light also, and we grow in our understanding of the Plan and how to work with it and bring it into existence. We are all growing and learning, and we learn from you just as you learn from us. We need your love just as you need our love. There needs to be a continual flow of love in both directions from the spiritual plane into the physical Earth and from the physical Earth back to the spiritual plane.

You can be a part of that movement. You can help to keep that flow going which allows the Plan to come to the Earth and to be a part of your life. Through maintaining this flow within you, you provide a vehicle for bringing the New Age about on the Earth and making it real now. We have all come far together and yet there is much left to do. We ask you to accept our guidance and that of your souls with the trust that we want what is best for you, and that we also want to achieve the same things that you do for yourselves and for the Earth. I promise you, no prayer ever goes unanswered for someone who is willing to accept the wisdom of our help and the loving understanding with which we seek to guide you now.

Thank you for your attention. Thank you for being here. Thank you for your love. Thank you for allowing us to be a part of your movement into the New Age now.

My love to you.

Exercise

Imagine you are flying. You are above the tallest trees, buildings, or mountains. You can see clearly everything that is going on but you are moving faster and faster. Your perception of what is happening around you can keep up with your movement so there is no blurring or confusion. You can record whatever images you wish for later recall. You can see in as great or as small a perspective as you want.

The faster you move the lighter you feel. And everything around you becomes lighter also. You begin to feel more radiant. There is an aura of light and love around you. You are aware of some divine presence in this light although it does not have a form that you recognize. Somehow this presence feels familiar. It is part of you. Allow its light to flow into you as you continue to move with it. The light feels good. It is energizing and calming at the same time. It feels like love flowing from your heart. This love wants to expand and flow unlimitedly.

Allow your heart to continue flowing the love as you focus again toward the Earth. Some places will support the love flowing through you. Their beauty and light blend with yours and there is more light around you. Other places might seem to draw your energy without giving any back. Allow your love to flow into these places until they seem to be full. Since you are constantly receiving energy as light and love from the divine presence accompanying you, you do not feel any loss. You only feel the love flowing and flowing, endlessly, unlimitedly.

Don't try to analyze the needs of any particular place you see, just share your love with it. Find the areas on Earth that wish to share beauty and love with you and share your light and love where it is needed. I will be there with your own divine presence to help you make the connections into this light-love flow that you need to make a positive difference on the Earth.

When you feel you are finished, fly back to your room and your place of meditation. Take your divine presence with you and feel it still surrounding you and filling your room with light. Feel its energy still flowing as love through your heart. Know that it is always there for you.

Archangel Sandalphon

Seeing Yourself as Light

Greetings to you, loved ones. My sphere of influence is the physical plane of the Earth. I embody all the Nature Spirits which you call elves, fairies or nymphs. They are all a part of my energies. My task is to harmonize the energies within physical existence and help it to receive the light of the higher planes and to evolve as light to a higher plane. I am working now to aid humanity in connecting the higher rays into the Earth itself and into their own physical structures, so that these higher rays will aid them in moving forward in their evolutionary path.

Light is the tool which you use to evolve. Light brings you everything that you need from the Creator. It is the creative tool you work with, and it embodies the result of your creative endeavor. The ultimate creative task for all of you in physical existence is to create for yourselves a physical body that is increasingly a tool for creating with light. It is your task to transform your physical structure from the lower vibrations of physical matter into ever increasing vibrational rates of finer physical material. Eventually, the atomic particles from which your physical structure is built will all be of light.

When you become all light and are aware of it consciously, you become powerful transmitters of light for the Earth. You become the clearest lenses possible for the creative focus of the Plan which Source intends for the Earth. You are able to read the Plan clearly without distortions from misunderstandings and misperceptions. You can radiate that light clearly as perfect beings who know consciously, and within your hearts, that you are of the same substance as your Creator. You will know consciously and within your heart that you are the Creator.

You are all radiating more light now than you realize. Everyone on Earth is using light more than ever before. If you could go back in time, you would find that human beings seemed darker and denser then than they do now. If you had etheric vision, you would be able to see even more clearly the difference.

That "something" which is so different is the new level which the Earth has reached. It is the new level of light and the new higher vibrations which have already become a part of physical existence.

Physical existence will continue to raise its vibrational level. It will be helped by each of you as you continue to clear yourself and to accept more and more light. You aid the whole of humanity and the whole of the Earth by raising the level of light which it expresses.

The greatest service that you can perform for the Earth or for humanity now is to learn to see light in everything that is around you. In everything you do, see yourselves as light. As you think so shall you be. You will gradually allow yourself through this exercise to become, more and more, light. You will not lose your physical structures through this. You will not float away or disintegrate. You will remain focused in physical existence because you desire to do so, and you hold a mental and spiritual concept of yourselves within a physical structure.

What you are doing now is learning to transform that mental concept into a physical structure that is composed of light rather than dense physical particles. This light structure still has a specific framework and still retains an individual form. At the same time, the light of which you are composed will be more radiant, and more responsive to all of those around you and to the spiritual energies that are coming to the Earth. Therefore, you will be able to share more clearly the joy, the love and the light that you receive.

I am also working very closely now with Metatron to link physical existence into the highest levels of the cosmic light which is available to Earth. You can use my energies as a link into the Earth and into your own creative expression within physical existence as divine light beings.

I am always available to aid you and support you in any way I can. If you have difficulty accepting your place on the Earth, or if you feel there is no place for you on the Earth or that you do not fit into humanity, ask for my help. I will help you find your place and help you discover how you fit into the Plan for the Earth.

You have a part in the Plan for the Earth or you would not be here. Your soul has a specific purpose within physical existence. It wants this physical experience very much. When you learn to express the light of the soul within you, and when you learn to be light on the Earth, then you will have available to you all the joy and love that is part of this light. Within light there is no darkness, no despair, no loneliness, and no fear. Within light there is joy, love, belonging, support by the whole, and freedom to grow as a creative being. This is all available to you as a part of physical existence. I would very much like to help you appreciate the wonderful opportunity that is yours as a part of physical existence.

Thank You. My love to you now.

Part III

DEVELOPING YOUR SPIRITUAL CONNECTION INTO THE PLAN

Exercise

Make a list of goals that you have for yourself. They may be practical or not, just things you would like to have or accomplish. Which three do you think are more important? Mark them with an "M" for mental. Which three seem more important from a viewpoint of physical security and support? Mark these "P." Which three are important to having fun and feeling good about yourself? Mark these "E" for emotional. Which ones feel more important if you look at them from your heart's perspective? Mark these "H." If you don't have three in each category, don't worry. Just check them off as you see best at this moment.

Take one from each category and see if they fit together in any way. How could you use them as components of your life and its direction? Think about how you might use them as thoroughly as you can, until your mind can go no further. Then let go of everything completely. Ask your soul for its guidance in this matter. Don't seek any particular direction, just allow a flow of thought from your soul. Some of what passes through your mind will seem like old thoughts but some will be new and will give you a new perspective on your direction and purpose.

Look at your list again. Is anything less or more important than it was before? If so, you have received spiritual help from your own inner guidance system.

Master Djwhal Khul

Cooperating with the Plan

I am very glad to have this opportunity to speak to you. I am called "The Messenger" within the Hierarchy. Much of my work has been to keep specific channels of communication open within the Hierarchy, and particularly between the Hierarchy and humanity. I work in the second ray, the Love-Wisdom Department, which is also the department of the World Teacher, the Christ. Therefore, I do much work for Him by disseminating the teachings to you that he feels are needed on the Earth now.

I've spent many lifetimes in Tibet as well as in the rest of the world. My last lifetime was as a Tibetan Monk, and that body is one I used for some time after I left physical existence. Although I am no longer using it, I may possibly go back to it again in the future.

I work very closely with the Master Kuthumi because he is my teacher along with the Christ. I also work very closely with the Master El Morya and Master St. Germaine. We work closely and very intensely to bring a body of information to the Earth that will help to create a New Age way of thinking. This is a way of thinking that allows each individual to recognize his own divine potential, and to recognize the importance of developing his creativity but, at the same time, to encourage cooperation at every level of the Plan and at every level of human endeavor.

Cooperation, I would say, is the most important thing you are working on now. We are seeking to help humanity see their similarities rather than their differences, and to help them work together as a group for a single purpose, rather than as a group of individuals each working for their own purposes and in conflict with one another. I have had a great deal to do with organizing the information that is given in this particular book. I do this quite often with other channeled works. I do not dictate the whole body of information, but I communicate and work with those who do, so that the necessary information is given. Then the Hierarchy finds the vehicles to bring Its knowledge and viewpoints to the Earth.

Every time we become aware of those who are writing a book or who are open to giving out this information in some way, we work with them, their soul or the teacher who is channeling through them to coordinate our efforts. In this way we can all combine our efforts to the best advantage. This book is part of a plan of awakening this New Age way of thinking, just as any book written under the guidance of a spiritual teacher is.

Now, there is another way to receive this information and to be guided into the New Age way of thinking other than by reading books. That is by developing your own inner connection and your own spiritual channel. The development of channeling on the Earth is a very important part of what we in the department of the world teacher are seeking to bring to the Earth. Each individual must learn to decide for himself what is appropriate. Each individual must learn to connect spiritually with the information that is most helpful to him.

The Plan needs many interpretations. No one within physical existence, I repeat, no one, is able fully to comprehend the complete spectrum of the intricacies and possibilities of the Plan. Even we, your spiritual teachers, do not claim to understand it completely. Each of us as a creative individual interprets it in his or her own way as best we can and contributes to it on that basis. In this way, there is a diversity and a richness, a completeness that comes into the Plan from the input of many individuals rather than just one. I would like to say here that we respect your creative viewpoint, your creative interpretation, just as much as we do ours. Our purpose is to help you stimulate that creativity, and to formulate that interpretation in line with your own divine purposes, as well as help you to develop it in alignment with the Divine Plan for the whole.

In order to be a clear channel for the Plan, and for this New Age way of thinking, you need to work continually on clearing the misperceptions within yourself. Balance various aspects of yourself which sometimes have come into conflict, and which prevent a clear flow of the light through you. There must be a constant searching within yourself for what needs to be released and what needs to be changed. There needs to be a continual openness to accepting the change within self and to accepting a newer, different viewpoint. Each time you reach a new level of understanding, that new level is merely a foundation for the next level of understanding which you will move to. As soon as you reach a new level, you must begin to release it.

There is a continual process of completion and then releasing in order to open to a new level of understanding. This requires you to be a person who is willing to learn from every part of your life, from every experience. You must be willing to look at yourself very objectively and very deeply, but still with great love and acceptance of yourself as well as of others. Through this process you continually clear your divine channel and more and more light becomes available to you within the flow of your physical existence as well as your spiritual existence. This may sound like a lot of work and not particularly fun and, perhaps, it is hard work. It's not easy to look at yourself with a very objective viewpoint and admit that there are things that need to be changed or things you need to do differently. However, the more you do this, the more light will come through as a result, and the more joyous will be your use of the light as you bring through more to the Earth.

This flow of light eventually brings out a clearer communication between your physical self and your spiritual self, and allows the mental and emotional selves to be a balanced part of that flow, which supports rather than blocks and distorts the flow of the light through you. This light is the means of manifesting the Divine Plan, the New Age on the Earth.

Another key to developing your channel is knowing when to communicate with us. I would like to say that the time just prior to the full moon and shortly thereafter is a time when the spiritual channels into the physical level are particularly open. This is a time when we seek most intensely to communicate with the Earth. This is a special time for alignment between the Hierarchy and humanity. It's not that we cannot bring you messages at other times, but simply that the flow is easier for you to connect into and easier for us to utilize at this time. I would recommend that at the time of the full moon you try to maintain an openness to communications, not necessarily from us, but perhaps for your higher self. Then, when it is appropriate, when your higher self has seen that you are balanced enough to be able to receive a communication from the spiritual teachers, they will help you make that connection and they will help you to bring through the message that you need.

The message need not be a very complicated one. It may be a simple statement of something that you need to work on right now. It may simply point out the answer to a question that you've been looking for. It might be a suggestion for some activity that will be helpful for you to engage in at that particular time to develop your strengths and to open new opportunities for service.

We are looking for people who are willing to serve and willing to work for the whole rather than for themselves. I would suggest that you look at service from the viewpoint of how you can fit into the whole rather than what it will do to benefit you. When you focus into yourself, you literally stop the flow. When you focus your desires into utilizing your energy in a group or for the benefit of the Earth there is a flow through you that brings more light and the assistance that you need. It also allows you to be more productive and to actually accomplish what the light is seeking to bring through you.

Simply focusing on how you can serve will allow you to be more loving, more joyous, more peaceful and more able to handle the difficulties that may arise. It is not focusing on being loving that teaches you to love. It is through desiring to serve, to help others and through allowing yourself to love them. When you create the channel for love by desiring to use it, you will receive all the love that you need, and you will have all of the love that you need to share. Act as if you are using love and you will find that you are love. So, it goes with all of the other heart qualities you are learning to develop now as a part of your evolution as a cocreator.

Well, getting the New Age movement going is a very serious affair. It requires much determined effort by each one of you. But it does not need to be so serious that there is no joy and no laughter. It's good to laugh and it is joy that is really the lubricant that allows the Plan to flow more easily. So don't allow yourself to get engrossed in serious work with an unhumorous approach to service. Allow yourself to see the joy and the laughter that is everywhere around you and make it a point to share these whenever possible.

Joy is a natural partner with love and light. It comes about from true knowledge of the real meaning of being spiritual. When you are actively working to become a part of the Plan and to improve your possibilities for service, we note the progress you are making and will send you whatever help you need. You do not have to ask. If you do invoke this help, it will be easier for you to connect into it. We are always here. Our purpose is to serve as consultants in the bringing forth of a more ideal way of experiencing physical existence.

We are not here to do it for you but we will do everything we can to help you understand the Plan, your part within it and how you can best serve to bring it forth now. This help is registered within you as an intuition, a clear knowing and a sureness about what you are doing that comes from the soul and from your heart. This inner knowing is much more valuable to you than the ability to literally receive a message from us. Anyone can receive a message, accurate or inaccurate, but a person who is developing spiritually knows and understands what that message means and is able to act upon it.

We ask that you allow your soul to become a part of your life, so that it can provide for you this inner knowing and the sureness that allows you to be in alignment with the Plan and with your own purposes without conscious effort. I am seeking to show you a little bit more realistic a viewpoint of what it means to work with the spiritual teachers and what it means to receive guidance from them. I hope that you will benefit from what I have been bringing to you here.

I am very grateful for this opportunity to speak with you and I thank you very much. My love to you.

Meditation

There is at least one special connection for you in my fleet and I would like to help you make it. Go through your channel if you can or make the connection to me as suggested in my message. You may feel an energy shift or receive some indication that something in you is a little different. There will be another shift as I help you meet and link up with your special friend and guide. Imagine that your friend is sitting beside you and loves you very much. He/she already knows many of your problems as well as your strengths. He or she will have a message for you and will be available for you again. You can discuss anything you like with your friend and receive guidance or new ideas.

If you are having trouble opening to your spiritual channel, you may not be aware of anything happening as you make this connection. Your subconscious may let you know about it in a dream. Pay attention, also, to small things that happen during the day which can reveal that something new is present in your life. If you have a lot of blocks to these new inner connections, you will have to be patient with yourself and validate them bit by bit. Your spiritual friends will be helping even though you are not always aware of them. Keep opening to the connection and trust that it is there.

If it is not always as clear as you would like, it will get better with use. Don't be afraid to ask for confirmation if you get something that doesn't feel right or make practical sense. Sometimes it takes a while to get the whole message through the misperceptions in your subconscious. Seeking truth will always help you find the correct answer. Loving and respecting yourself will allow you to receive valid guidance.

Commander Soltaan

Receiving Help through the Plan

I, Commander Soltaan, am bringing you the light of a thousand galactic suns, the suns of this galaxy. I am here as the leader of a large group of beings, a collection of energies, which is focused within the creative core of this galaxy. We are helping to flow to you the Plan and the knowledge about that core which will help you build a new Earth. We bring the many resources of light that you need to move forward in your evolution and the vision of what the Earth will be into a reality.

We work with light and the essence of light. We work with the motivating force of light which is the creative flow. We interpret this light through our understanding of it, and then focus that understanding to you as a framework of ideas which you can connect into and use as inspiration for your work on the Earth. You might say that we are a vast reservoir of creative ideas which are potentialities for your world now. The light that we project carries the Plan for an ideal Earth and for a New Age which will allow each of you to live in the way which seems most satisfying to you as creators.

You can attune to these ideas and make use of them by allowing the light of the Galactic Core to become a part of your life, a part of your mental, emotional and physical structure, through your soul. Your soul (spiritual) structure is already aligned with it and it is through this connection that you will be able to bring it into your conscious awareness.

You may not be aware that you are making the connection through your soul, but if that is your intention, and if you continue to allow it, the connection and the awareness of it will become stronger and stronger within you. This will give you the confidence that you need to allow a continuous flow of this supportive energy and light, which is available from the Galactic Center.

If you attune to my ship or to me, I can help you make a connection through your soul, so you can receive the light and this knowledge into your mind and heart and use it from your heart. What you learn from the spiritual side of life must come through your heart. It is interpreted by your mind and it is formed into a conceptual framework which is usable on the Earth, but it must make a connection into your heart before it can actually flow into the physical part of your life and become a reality on the Earth plane.

Those who work with me on my ship are specifically trained to help you make this connection. We are what you might call "Cosmic Psychologists." We understand how your mind and emotional processes work so we can help you utilize that mental-emotional structure that you do have and help you clear it. In this way, we can help you develop the ability to use the cosmic potentialities that are within you, as a tool to bring this Cosmic Plan to the Earth.

We are already working with many of you on the inner planes while you sleep or during your meditations. You may not always be aware that we are there. You may be focusing on some other individual who is helping you to make a connection into the Galactic Center but we are also there with you. This connection with us is something that you have chosen at a soul level and are now using at that level, but it is enhanced and vitalized when you are able to attune to it consciously.

For many of you, merely reading these words will be enough to help you make the connection. For others of you it might look like a good idea but one which you aren't really ready to accept right now. In this case, I can assure you that you have already made the connection on the inner side and are merely waiting for the courage to allow it to come forth on the outer. First, you must release the fear which prevents you from recognizing this connection. If you know that we are love, that we come with love and that we come with respect for your right to make your own choices, you will understand that nothing is being forced upon you and that we help only when we have been asked and when we are allowed to come into your heart.

Through those who already have connections with me and individuals in my fleet, we are bringing to the Earth techniques for working with the emotional body. We work to balance it, to clear it and to release it from the bondage of lower emotions which are not helpful for your progress right now. We are also bringing techniques to help you recognize and utilize the many positive emotions which you have developed and are now ready to use more and more in achieving your purposes on the Earth. Some of these higher emotions such as unlimited love, joy, peace, the desire to serve are the links to the Cosmic Plan and into the network of energies which are available to create the New Age on your Earth. These higher emotions are the vital flow which allows you to communicate not only with the spiritual planes but with those within your own plane who are your co-workers or cocreators with you of this New Age.

We are bringing techniques to help you release the fears and blocks that hinder your working with others in a group. We also want to help you learn to work with those of us on the inner planes who are not a part of physical existence, but who are here to help you. We can help you release your fear and resistance to being a part of the Earth itself so you can make a clear, flowing connection into the Earth as part of spiritual existence. This allows you to bring that Plan forth into the physical Earth instead of just leaving it to exist as a fantasy in your minds. We are interested in achieving practical results. We are working to help you bring to the Earth practical solutions for working out the Divine Plan within a physical environment which does not now appear to be ready to accept it. We are helping you to prepare the Earth to receive this better way, this New Age, which will bring much joy and a satisfying spiritual experience.

I would be delighted to speak with you through your own inner channel at any time. Imagine a flow of energy coming to you from it. Know at the same time that this energy is actually flowing from a point above the top of your head or, perhaps more accurately, into the center of your head from a point all around you. Begin by asking to feel my energy around you, and then allow that energy to come into your body. It will come gradually and gently so as not to frighten you. Give yourself a few minutes to make this connection and allow this supportive energy structure to form around you, and then begin to allow that to focus within your head and heart.

Each of you will experience the connection according to your own particular abilities and level of communicative awareness. Some of you may see colors, a form, or even a face. Others may hear a voice. Others may sense a message. Many of you will think that you are merely making this up in your mind but if you receive a message in your mind record it in some way. Say it into a tape recorder or write it down. When you look at it again after you have come out of your meditation, I think you are very likely to see that it is something that came from outside your mind and is something that was not there before. In this way you can begin to develop the ability to communicate through your mind and through your channel. Allow the energy connection to be made within your heart so that you feel secure there, and then it will come more easily into your mind.

I'm looking forward to hearing from you. There are many on my ship and in my fleet who are ready to communicate with you, and to help you in any way that is appropriate for you now.

Thank you very much. My love and the love of all those who are here with me is flowing to you. Please accept it.

Exercise

Make a large triangle, at least twelve inches per side, all sides equal, out of white paper or cardboard. In the center make a large, bright blue circle with a silver spot in the center. This will serve as a focus for meditation.

When you meditate, place the triangle about eighteen inches in front of your eyes and look at it. Imagine a line of energy coming from the silver spot to the center of your forehead. Imagine the blue surrounding your head and the white surrounding your whole body. This forms an energy space which facilitates your communication with us and protects you from outside interference.

We have many ideas we would like to share with you to make the flow of your life a more productive part of the Divine Plan and to help you channel your creative potential into a more satisfying life on Earth. Try out our energy space and allow us to share our love with you through our combined creative potential.

Commander Soltec

Humanity's Responsibility
to Change the Earth

My warmest greetings to you, friends of the Earth and friends in the light. I am the commander of a large fleet of 5,275 mother ships under the Ashtar Command. Within these mother ships are countless other smaller ships that we use to continually patrol the Earth, to monitor specific ones of you who are our friends and whom we are assisting in your work on the Earth. We also provide specific services for the Earth itself, if they do not interfere with your free will and your opportunity to create your own destiny. We are here to help in every way that we can but we will not interfere with what you have created.

We insist that you be allowed to solve your own problems and develop the Earth as you choose to create it. This may sound rather harsh. You say, "I'm not the one who is polluting the Earth. I'm not the one who is building bombs. I'm not the one who is killing anyone." But you are a part of humanity and you are a part of the consciousness which is creating this. Therefore, since you have chosen to come and work within it, it is up to you to change it from within.

The mass consciousness of the Earth cannot be changed from without any more than the beliefs of a human being can be changed from without. These changes must come from within. They must be experienced by the individual or the group involved, and must be worked out in the consciousness of each one.

That doesn't mean we can do nothing for you. We are here to help you bring in light when you desire to work on your own physical bodies and to perfect them, so they can be the light they truly are. We have hospital ships that are specifically designed to help you perfect your physical structures. We can bring your etheric bodies up here at night and work to clear them or to heal them. If this is accepted by your consciousness, it will directly affect your physical level.

If enough people desire certain information, and if the whole seems to be ready for it, we can send that information to individuals who are capable of receiving it. Some of them will be able to bring the information through from their higher mind, and create the structure or device for work in developing the group awareness which is desired. We have some specific devices or machines on our ships which are particularly helpful for sending information and for sending the type of healing rays, for instance, which are needed.

We have ships which are devoted entirely to cleaning up the atmosphere and removing those combustible particles from atomic radiation that are so dangerous for the existence of your planet. We also have machines that are working to replenish the ozone layer of the planet and to balance the ionization of the particles within certain strata of Earth's atmosphere.

We also have ships that work under the seas to keep the acid balance of the oceans within reasonable limits. The pollution, the radiation, and the damage done by some naturally occurring events within the Earth's crust can cause that to become dangerously out of balance. As a result, all of the life within and around the oceans becomes threatened. It is understood on your planet that trees play a very important part in supplying the vital gases which you need to breathe in your atmosphere, but it is not known how much your oceans contribute to a healthful atmosphere for humanity and the rest of the life on the planet.

We have received special permission from the Hierarchy of your planet to carry out some of these tasks because it really is necessary to provide an Earth fit for humanity's existence. In other words, we are buying you some time and giving you a little more room to "get your act straightened out" so you can heal Earth, continue to live on it and explore the marvelous potentials it has for you to be creative in it. Without the help that we have offered you so far, your Earth would be much less livable than it is now.

Your Earth is an especially beautiful planet. I have seen many and there are few that come near the incredible beauty of its seas, its plants, its beautiful atmosphere and the light that it radiates. The Earth itself is a beautiful being who is developing her creativity, just as you are, and who desires to work with humanity and all of her kingdoms to create a beautiful experience to share with Source. She wishes more and more to share herself with the galaxy. The Earth, and those of you within humanity who are working for the light, are invoking light that has not been available before.

This light that is coming to you now, as other teachers have told you, contains the blueprint for the New Age. It contains also the blueprint for a new humanity. This is a humanity that will not know cruelty or war or selfishness. These traits are now being removed from your genetic structure as you submit to the help we can give you.

The most important thing for you is to see that it is possible to eliminate war and hunger and lack of freedom. You must learn to live without the expectations of these in your own life and to clear your own consciousness of everything which allows these. Then you become tools for bringing through a clear vision of what life on the Earth can be. When you bring through this clearer vision, the negative conditions that are present on the Earth will no longer affect you. You will become positive forces for changing the Earth. These changes will offer much positive growth and help for your suffering planet and all its suffering life forms.

I have spent many lifetimes on the Earth, some in Atlantis, many in Lemuria and many in times before that. I have spent time studying at the university on Sirius and in the temples at the Galactic Center. I have visited many planets in this galaxy and throughout the universe through many lifetimes. I have served the Earth in this physical body for about 500 years and I am planning to stay around for at least 500 more. I love the Earth very much. All of us do. We feel a great desire to aid her in any way we can.

Although we are not in dense physical existence itself, we feel very much a part of the Earth and part of what she is trying to become. All of you who are working for the light have many friends in our ships. They are always available for you when you need them. When you offer a prayer or ask for divine assistance there will always be someone there for you. There will probably be more help available for you than you can recognize or use. If you cannot directly perceive this, or if you don't feel you can understand it fully yet through your intuition, trust that it is there. Continue to seek this understanding and it will come.

Each one of you is capable of communicating with us. Each one of you can learn to become a very clear channel for the information and the energy that we bring to the Earth. We invite you to use this connection. We invite you to visualize our ships in your mind sending you a beam of loving energy, which can support you and the Earth in many ways, if you will allow us, and if you will align with those energies that come to you.

As your friend and your teacher, I am available to you any time you wish to speak with me. I have great love for you, and I would like an opportunity to share it with each one of you. I thank you for your loving service, and the light which you share with all around you.

Exercise

Take a walk someplace where you will meet many people. You don't have to know them. Make direct eye contact with as many as possible and give a simple greeting. This will be easy for some of you and very difficult for others. (It gets easier as you discover that many people respond very positively. All won't but you don't need to worry about that.) As you greet them, imagine they are made of light and their light is all around them. The more light you see in them, the more light you will feel in yourself.

This sounds very simplistic but it can have profound effects on your ability to achieve any creative purpose in your life. We will be with you, greeting them on more subtle levels, sharing our love with them as well as with you.

Nascia

Bringing New Ideas to Earth

My friends, I am a part of the communications network at the Galactic Center. My job is to oversee communicative connections that are being made to the Earth at many levels. I oversee the communications to the galactic fleet that is stationed around the Earth. I help to establish some of the communicative links between members from the Galactic Center departments to Earth.

There is much knowledge here that we wish to transmit directly to the Earth from the Galactic Center. There are some of you who are already receiving information from the commands and from your Hierarchy. You and others have come to Earth with the specific purpose of establishing a link between the Galactic Center and the Earth.

The purpose of this link is to allow humanity to experience a deeper sense of its own spiritual heritage, a deeper sense of the extent of their divinity and how far they can progress as cosmic beings now. We have information to bring to the Earth on spiritual matters, what you call philosophy. We have other material in the form of scientific concepts and specific inventions which will be of great value to your Earth and of great help to you as you seek to learn to live more in harmony with the Earth Itself. We will be bringing you the knowledge you need to build environmentally safe power sources, healing techniques and new methods of food production. We also bring methods of working within self to balance the emotional body and to help you to communicate more clearly with your own soul aspects.

We use specific devices here similar to radio broadcasters and receivers which help us to connect with the individual who is receiving the message. We can tune our "broadcasting system" to the specific vibrational input frequency of the channel with whom we are communicating. This helps them receive the information more clearly. This is not always done initially and it is not being done as I bring this message to you now.

For those of you who seek a contact and allow it and who continually attune to it, we will be able to intensify and clarify the connection by utilizing our radio devices. For some it will not be necessary. For some it will be extremely helpful when we bring through much more specific information such as actual diagrams and charts. I am telling you this because I would like to connect in with some of you who have agreed to do this at another level and who have consciously realized within your physical vehicle that this is one of your purposes.

This message to you will help open your conscious awareness to this possibility and, perhaps, encourage you to develop the inborn talents you have brought to Earth. Virtually all of the great inventions that are being used on Earth now to make your lives easier have been brought to the Earth from the inner planes by those who were able to receive the message. That is how the Galactic Center will continue to bring information to you that you can use to improve your lives, and your ability to control and create your environment to your liking and in a way that is beneficial to the Earth as well. If you choose to attempt this communication, you may attune to me, and I will refer you to the appropriate individual who is ready to work with you. If you do not feel a connection right away, simply persist and, eventually, you will begin to recognize that a connection had indeed been made. It's as if you ring a bell and we immediately recognize your desire to make that connection. However, you do not always allow yourselves to receive the answer or the return communication. Even though a message is being sent you may have a little difficulty receiving it clearly at first. Practice will help you perfect this method of communicating with another being through your mind and through your spiritual awareness.

For some of you, a regular program of practicing and attunement will be all that is necessary for you to make this connection. Others of you may need the help of those who teach channeling, or who can offer you some advice on how to make the connection. For a start, I would advise that you simply visualize a point directly overhead, and send a stream of golden light from the center of your head up to that point and recognize that it is the Galactic Center. This initiates an energy flow that connects you with us.

For those who wish to attune to the Galactic Center, and are not a part of the program of bringing through inventions, there is a teacher here who can help you with your spiritual development and with using other talents. The Galactic Center would like to help you to develop these in order to assist in connecting the light of the Central Sun into the Earth itself.

Your purpose, or your mission, is always chosen with regard for your abilities and the knowledge that you have developed within physical existence. You will not be asked to do anything that is too difficult or impossible but only what is needed for what you are developing within yourself on the Earth, and what will also aid you in your evolution now.

We seek to support the forward movement of the Earth and every individual within humanity. If you can attune consciously to every avenue of help that is available to you, your spiritual growth will move much more rapidly.

Already on your planet there are more and more individuals becoming aware that there is such a place as the Galactic Center. Although many of you are not quite sure where the beings you communicate with are coming from, you are already receiving valuable help and guidance.

There are many teachers and workers here who wish to make this connection into the Earth through a member of humanity. They can facilitate your work and move the growth of the whole galaxy forward. For as your Earth grows, and as each of you grows, so do we all grow.

Meditation

Imagine a tube of golden light, big enough to go around your head. This light tube goes up to the higher levels of consciousness where only truth exists and also goes through you into the earth. I am at the top of this tube pouring buckets of gold and silver sparkles through it. The sparkles dance joyously, touching every speck of negativity they meet, turning it into light. Let the tube expand a bit so your body is within it and you can take a light shower.

I will be having enormous fun sending you this bright, joyful energy. I want to help you feel the joy, acceptance and love that can be yours if you allow it. I will be trying to make you laugh and have fun. Being full of light is much nicer than not. You can use this tube as a channeling connection or just to feel good. I hope you will try it.

Alazaro

Friends in Service to Earth

Greetings to you, my dear ones. I am very glad to have this opportunity to speak with you. I have been a member of the Angelic Kingdom and worked with some of you within physical existence from that perspective. I have enjoyed that experience very much. I have been so fascinated by what all of you are doing and learning and becoming that I have asked and been allowed to transfer from the Angelic Kingdom to the human kingdom. As I work with your spiritual teachers, and your Planetary Hierarchy itself I have already begun to work toward that end. I have begun to prepare the physical body which I will enter into at that time.

I have worked with many other planets and galaxies but I have been particularly fascinated by your beautiful and very loving Earth. I have been captured by a desire to work with her in as complete a way as I can. It seems to me that becoming a conscious creator and becoming a part of physical existence would be the way in which I could be of most service to her, and also the way in which I could learn more about this Earth experience.

For some time I have been working with many of you, particularly in developing your channeling, and that is something which I hope to be able to continue. It is very important now for all of you to be able to get in touch with your own inner selves and with the help that is available to you through that inner self.

Through the channeling process, I have seen many of you come to a much greater realization of your own potentials, and I have seen you establish a much greater connection with your own souls. I have seen you grow much faster as spiritual beings because of these connections. This growth within you is causing a similar growth within the planet. You are a part of the Earth, and every step which you take becomes a step for the Earth also.

So many of you are now taking these steps into your own unlimitedness that you are really helping to move the Earth forward much faster than it ever has before. Many of us have seen that your Earth has a desire to be loving and of service to all of its kingdoms and to the solar system. Your Earth is eager now to move forward, to learn to love more clearly, to work more creatively, and to produce a creative experience that will truly show what source beings can do.

I am very excited about being a part of this now, and being able to work with so many of you also. I would like to help you with your channeling. I would like to be able to help you make that connection with your higher self, which will allow you to make further connections to all of the wonderful teachers who are available to you. The way you channel is not important. The fact that you are able to make this connection is important, and that you are able to allow it to flow through you to the Earth.

One of my particular strengths has been said to be a quality of "flowing," and I would like to help all of you learn to flow with the tide that is moving the Earth now. This is a tide of light, a flow of light, that is moving faster and faster, giving you the opportunity to move into alignment with it in a way that allows you to become more light.

Now, you are already light beings, although you haven't always understood that. As you align with the light, and allow yourselves to move with it, you will become more aware of how much you are like this light flow and how much you are able to be a part of it. This flow is moving you into a more expanded communion with all of those around you. At the same time, it is moving you into an expanded vision of what you are as an individual being. It's moving you into a greater understanding of your creative potentials and is increasing your cosmic awareness of yourselves. From my unique perspective, I think I can help you connect into that part of yourself which is divine, which is Source. Then you can align that Source perspective with that part of yourself which seeks to learn and become a conscious creator who understands his special talents as an individual.

I would like to become friends with you and talk with you. When we are comfortable with each other, I can help you to make a connection to other teachers and to learn to move and flow as you allow the message they have for you to come through.

I would also like to aid you in channeling energy from many spiritual sources into the Earth itself. I would like to help you make a spiritual connection with your beautiful Earth so you can relate to her as one light being to another. Allow me then to be your friend and allow me to share your consciousness from time to time, in a meditation or in a friendly conversation. I would appreciate that very much. I would hope to be able to serve you by helping you "tune in" more clearly to the many opportunities that are available to you through the spiritual teachers or through your inner selves.

✧ Part IV

RECOGNIZING YOUR POTENTIAL

Exercise

Think of an instance where you suffered badly or came out on the worst end of a deal. You don't need to reexperience all the negative emotions you felt, but remember what they were and set them in front of you as if they were objects. Now imagine how it would be if things had worked out in your favor. Imagine the good feelings which would be in you. Ask your heart to make them yours. Reach out with it and take in the positive experience you have created. Let your heart expand with them and push out or dissolve the negative ones.

Ask your soul and one of us, I will be glad to help, to support you in forgiving yourself for the negative experience. Ask for love and light to transform it into the positive one. Let the image and emotions of the positive experience flow into every part of your body. Check specific areas to make sure they will take it. If one seems stuck, ask for a special energy boost to clear that area. Take a moment to look at what you have done when our energy is part of your perspective.

Know that you are forgiven all mistakes. Know that any experience can be enriching if you learn from it. All action moves energy. Let your actions now bring in more positive reactions than before. Trust yourself to always move forward into greater wisdom and ability to use love. Put these affirmations into the path which moves forward from your reconstructed experience. Think of them as your next experience takes shape. When you act with love, I will be with you.

Sananda

Joy in Love

Greetings, my friends. I bring my love to you. I am the one who is known to many of you as the Master Jesus but I have grown much since you knew me by that name. I have chosen this new name, Sananda, to represent an evolved picture of what I am now. Many of you imagine me to be very sober, serious and strict. But the need for that has long passed and now it is a time of joy, a time for experiencing your spirituality in a way that brings you enjoyment rather than suffering. It is no longer necessary to suffer on Earth to be spiritual or in order to bring light and love. The Earth is ready now to receive your light and your love in a joyous way that allows you to share the joy that has always been there.

My task on Earth has been to serve as a vehicle for that Christ consciousness which anchored love into your Earth as it had never been anchored before. My purpose was to help show that love can be a way of life on the Earth, that love is something to be desired and utilized creatively. However I was only the prototype. It is time now for the improved and perfected version of light bearers on the Earth. I am still working to help you do what I did in an even greater way. My department is working now through all religions of the world, and through all groups who come together to serve and bring light to the Earth. We will help all who work together to share their love of their Creator through their service on the Earth within physical existence.

It is time to put away images of the spiritual as being serious, strict, and existing solely for discipline. You have learned to control your emotions and to balance them with the mind and you are working to perfect that balance. It is time to allow the joy that is within your heart to come forward within this more balanced energy that you are projecting.

What better way to project joy than to feel within you the love of the Creator that has been placed there from your beginning? What better way than to just allow yourself to touch into the joy that is in you, and to feel it coming forth on the radiance of the love that is within you, and the light that is beaming forth from your heart?

I am still available to all of you whenever you seek to communicate with me or to feel my love which is always there for you. I hear your prayers, I see your light and I respect the spiritual purpose that is growing within you. If you allow me to come into your heart, I will help you discover the infinite love and the unlimited creative power that is there for you. I will help you to develop within yourself the ability to utilize this unlimited creative light that is yours through your connection to your Creator. Put away the need to be cheerless and let the joy of your love radiate from your being.

Let us also put away the need to judge ourselves and each other, and appreciate instead the light that is available in each. Release the unworthiness that you feel as physical beings, and allow yourself to see that you are truly unlimited spiritual beings with an enormous creative potential for joy. We are truly creating a planet of joy now. The New Age will be one where each can experience physical existence in a way that goes beyond what has previously been known on Earth, because it will combine the knowledge of joy, love and your own divine heritage.

The Earth is now a different Earth. We are all different beings, and now you can begin to experience the Earth and yourselves differently. You can begin to allow your light to bring you joy as it brings it to the Earth.

There are many of us here in the spiritual kingdom to support you in the Earth, to aid you in what you are doing there and to assist you in your growth and evolution. There are more of us in the spiritual planes than there are of you on the Earth, so you never need to feel a lack of spiritual support. There is more than enough for each of you if you can allow yourself to accept it, to trust it and to utilize the energy and the light that it can bring to you. Each time you attune to us and communicate with us we grow and learn, just as you grow and learn. Through your connections into the spiritual levels of being, you explore and see new potentials within yourself. We will help you to grow and expand your vision of yourself as a divine being.

It does not satisfy us in any way when you think of yourselves as less than us or less worthy of being light or less worthy of communicating with the spiritual energies that are available to you. What pleases us is to see you growing in your awareness of yourselves as divine beings, and growing in your ability to see the vast spiritual potential of each one of you.

Our purpose is to guide each of you and to guide the Earth itself into a greater awareness of its own light potential. We want to help you realize your full creative power. We want to help you clear yourselves of misperceptions about yourselves, so that you can be perfect channels for the Plan of the Creator. We want to help you to align yourselves with the will of the Creator so that you can appreciate the joy and the fulfillment that comes from aligning with that will. We want to help you see that you are a part of a group whose purpose is to serve the will of the Creator with joy, in light and through love.

Thank you.

Meditation

Get out your list of all your positive traits and strengths. See if you need to add anything new. Place each one in your heart and try to experience how each one feels and how it affects your thinking. Think about a time when you used it and it worked at least a little. As you validate each one and experience it, your heart will expand and feel lighter. These qualities are the energy spaces your soul needs to be part of your life. Offer yourself to it now, knowing that you have earned its participation with you. Just sit or lie quietly and allow it to be with you.

Nothing else is needed for now. Be one with your best self. It is the real you.

Raphael

Finding Your Divinity in Your Heart

I, Raphael, come to you with love and light to greet you as a part of Creation. You are a part of that light that is filling all of Creation with beauty and love. My special part in this Creation is to focus the consciousness of your own awareness of all that you are. This can help you consciously recognize the light and love within yourselves. You can utilize that knowledge in physical existence.

At this time my purpose here is to help you focus your divine beingness at the physical level, and see that you are not less divine because you are physical. I am a flow of light into your heart from Source Itself which allows you to express all of your light, all of your love, all of your joy, and all of the divine knowingness and unlimited knowledge that are within you. So, I can help you to use these in your life on the Earth. I am a part of this flow for the Earth too, as I seek to aid her in expressing her creative abilities and her divine knowingness into all that she is doing.

The Earth as a supporter and protector is working very hard now to become a cosmic supporter and protector of all of her children. She is seeking to bring more of this cosmic light into herself and seeking to share it with you. You can receive this light in many ways. You can receive it from your spiritual teachers, you can receive it from the Earth and you can receive it directly in your heart. An awareness of your unlimited creative abilities is already within your heart and available to you there. Many of us are helping you find it. We are tapping a source of unlimited love which supports and guides your creative contributions to the Earth. We want to help you use your heart as a connection into all of your creative potential.

I am a part of the Creator who knows only that I am a part of the Creator. I know nothing of separateness. I know nothing of darkness. I know only love, that is what I bring to you. That love reflects in many ways, it is projected as light, joy, beauty, harmony and as consciousness of that divinity that I am.

This unlimited awareness is available to you also, if you can allow yourselves to receive it while you are in physical existence. You already know this in that eternal part of yourselves, the seed of unlimited divine potential which is centered in your heart. It is that seed which we are now uncovering so that you can flower as unlimited creative beings on many levels of awareness. As conscious beings, you have the choice of aligning into this unlimited love or looking elsewhere for something to support your purpose.

Meditation

Imagine a disk of bright blue light about six inches over your head. There is a glow of golden light around it. Six inches under your feet there is another disk; this one is bright green and it radiates a deeper gold. The two disks are like a battery. The one over your head is the positive pole, the one under your feet is the negative one. They generate an electrical flow between them. The energy flows through your body into the earth.

You can put "dimmer switches" wherever you feel you need them. Most of you have at least a little fear of electricity so this will allow your subconscious mind, which has the job of protecting you, to feel better about this little exercise. Now ask your soul to send you the amount of light it feels you can handle at the moment. Use your switch to gradually increase the flow in a way that feels comfortable.

Now just sit and allow the flow. Adjust it when you feel it is necessary, but just allow it. Relax into it. Some will feel very light and tingle. Some may see light. Some may feel fears and doubts, not just about the exercise but about yourself. Allow whatever comes and let it flow electrically also. Some may feel nothing. Still trust that what you asked for is happening. Just be with this energy for at least five minutes.

After that you can begin to direct the energy from your heart to anything or anyone's image which you would like to help, heal, or activate. The light not only activates your power, it can show you places inside yourself which need work or which aren't being used. It will also connect you to your place in the Plan.

Serapis Bey

Working with Your Soul

Greetings, dear friends and co-workers. The name, Serapis Bey, was given to me during my last lifetime in the Mid-East. I am still very much interested in helping to work out problems in that area. However my work now entails the use of what I learned in my many lifetimes in every part of the Earth. I was a Roman king, a Grecian peasant, a Roman doctor and a Russian landowner. I was a slave in India in a very ancient part of your history. I have been a monk or a holy man in various eastern countries many times. I have spent many lifetimes in Africa and in South America. In other words, I have experienced many physical lifetimes on your Earth and have worked with many of you.

My job now is with the Third Ray Department of Earth's Spiritual Hierarchy. This department administers the flow of the Plan to the Earth. The third department energizes the Earth with light and its electrical potential. The job of this third department is to step down the spiritual light from the Hierarchical levels into a frequency which the physical aspects of the Earth can grasp and utilize.

In that sense, we are the ones who bring you the light that you are using in your lives. The second ray or the Christ Ray is the one that allows you to connect that light into your heart so that it is a part of you. The first ray is the one which helps you to direct your intentions so that you receive the connections that are desirable and in alignment with what you want to experience and accomplish on the Earth.

Many of us who have been presented in this book have said we are here to help you in any way that we can. We have told you how our light is available to you, and how it supports you, and helps you to understand your place on the Earth and within the Plan for the Earth. We serve as older friends, bigger brothers and sisters who have had a little more experience and have gained a little more wisdom in working with physical existence. We are willing, at all times, to share that with you.

I would like to emphasize now the importance of using your own soul for this purpose. Your soul is the part of you which is very intimately connected with your Planetary Hierarchy. Your soul is a part of the Planetary Hierarchy which allows you to share in the administration of this evolutionary movement on the Earth, which is being guided by the Plan. Your soul is what connects you into the Plan and what connects you to us, your spiritual teachers. It's the vehicle that you use to extend yourself into the fuller use of your divine potential. Your soul is literally a light garment which you can put on and wear inside and outside of yourself. It allows you a clearer connection into light on many levels and the full reality of what you are as a divine being.

This is the most important focus of the Plan right now. When we say we are anxious to help all of you expand the use of your creativity and to use your full potential on the Earth, what we are really saying is that we want you to integrate this light vehicle which is yours. It has access to your full potential and connects you to the purpose and the infinite creative ability which you are seeking to use on the Earth. This is the focus of the Plan perhaps more than anything else right now.

Your soul is that part of you that makes you one of us, that makes you our equal, and which allows you to function fully as a cocreator on the Earth. Until you can realize fully the potential of this light vehicle, you will not see fully the way to interact with others, with the Earth and with the Plan for the Earth which comes through us, your spiritual teachers. You are following a path on the Earth which allows you to find, bit by bit, more of the availability of this soul energy, more of the knowledge and understanding of how to interact with it and how to share with it your physical plane focus.

As you learn to see and use this light vehicle which is your soul, it allows you to establish the connections within yourself that provide communication at the inner levels with not only us, your teachers, but with others of humanity at the soul level. I am talking about a deeper level of communication. One that comes from using your heart, yes, but from using your heart as a focus of your soul's energies on the Earth.

Your heart is the focus of this light that is the soul. It is the connection point that holds the soul's energies within you. It is also the point from which your mind becomes illumined, and from which you learn to understand what it means to be light and what it means to be a part of a light structure that is evolving.

Your mind is important. Knowledge is important. Understanding and wisdom are ultimate qualities which you are seeking to integrate into your life. What I am saying is that you need to integrate all of this into a heart focus which allows the soul to guide you from the point of love, and which allows you to connect into the inherent knowledge that you have carried with you since you first incarnated as a physical being. This knowledge has always been there. It is what you are learning to use in physical existence. Let's say it is made available most completely and in the most balanced way, by allowing your soul to work with you and help you in that process.

You can't do it by yourself. There is no way. You must learn to accept the guidance of this other part of yourself, which sometimes seems like a foreigner or an outside entity that is going to come in and take from you everything that you have now. Through communication with your soul and through the utilization of the Christ energy to guide you in the acceptance of the use of your soul in your life, you get acquainted with it bit by bit. Gradually you learn to allow it more and more to be a part of your life until, finally, you can trust it to come into your life completely and to be a part of everything that you do.

This is not the place, I think, to go into all of the details of all that process involves. It is a lengthy one. It is something that you all have been working on for many lifetimes. That's normal. The important thing to know is that many of you have now reached the point where you are able to bring the soul's energies into your life and use them through a physical vehicle, that is more balanced in its physical, emotional, and mental aspects that it ever has been before. Thus you can learn to allow your soul to utilize this newly perfected vehicle in a way which will help you to align more clearly with the Plan, and more clearly with the divine purposes of those who are guiding the creative effort on the Earth.

As cocreators on the Earth you are a part of that Plan. You had a part in creating it and have chosen your part within the Plan. You have chosen the direction that the Earth is taking, and you have even chosen the problems which the Earth has been trying to resolve. This was done at the soul level. As you learn to bring your soul's light and understanding into your life, you are able to connect more clearly into the reasons behind what is going on around you.

As I said before, your soul is a part of the Hierarchy of the Earth. It's a part of the creative framework which is guiding it. Through your soul you become a part of this, a part of the decision-making process, as well as a part of the process which actively brings about the manifestation of this framework on the Earth. Your soul is what allows you to be a conscious and willing participant in the Plan, rather than simply a pawn within it. Your soul is what connects you into the light, and with the soul's light comes the understanding and the wisdom which allow you to be a conscious cocreator within the Plan and a dynamic cocreator within physical existence.

My message to you is a simple one. I want to assure you that there is a Plan, spiritual guidance, and a group of individuals here who have passed beyond the physical experience but who have remained to guide the Earth and to help you connect into the Divine Plan as it exists at less physical levels. I also want you to know that you are an integral part of this Plan, the builders of it. The mechanism by which you achieve this is your soul which is seeking more and more to become a part of your life on the Earth. Our purpose is to help you understand that, accept it and use it.

If we seem at times to suddenly pull away and expect you to do things yourself, it is because we see that you are able to utilize your own soul to accomplish what you are asking us to do. We cannot and will not do anything for you that you can do yourself because this would be denying you the opportunity to learn to use your own creative abilities. That doesn't mean that we don't remain with all the love and the light to support you. We are here as much as you will allow us and we have as much appropriate help as you are willing to accept. We are not in physical existence so we cannot manifest the Plan for physical existence against the will of those who are a physical part of it. Therefore it is your responsibility to finally bring the Plan to the Earth and to build it there. This will be done by those who are able to use their souls as their guides on the Earth and their connections into the light of the Plan.

As you make this soul connection and as you learn to use it more in every part of your life and to manifest it through your heart and through your illumined mind, the Plan begins to flow through you in a way that allows you to draw more light into yourself, and to draw from others the support you need to create that Plan. In other words, this light flow is an actual electrical flow which generates a magnetic field around it. This magnetism is the love that flows from one who is using the light, working with the soul and allowing the Plan to flow through him. When you can learn to function in this way clearly and consistently, your life begins to flow in a smooth and purposeful way. The light simply washes all of the problems away, and you begin to move forward on your path with surer footsteps. The path may appear to become a little steeper because there are more opportunities to serve but it becomes wider and easier to follow.

You have a marvelous opportunity to bring forth the divine ideal onto the Earth in a way that it has never functioned before, and we know that we, along with you, are going to be successful in accomplishing that.

I thank you very much for sharing your time and your love with me. Again, I offer my support in helping you grow in your use of your divine soul potentials. My love is with you always as part of the light which guides you along your spiritual path.

Meditation

Imagine a sphere of silver and blue light coming down around you. It surrounds you completely and penetrates your whole body, every cell. It dissolves all negativity, all pain, fear, anger, depression, sadness, guilt. It is loving and accepts you unconditionally. It strengthens all your positive feelings and the parts where there is already light. These expand and absorb or push out everything else.

The center of the light is in your heart center, in the star I mentioned before. The star expands and brightens as you recognize it there. When you have just enjoyed this for a while, you may be ready to speak with me. I will be glad to talk with you, help you with healing, or just be there for you. I bring you the Creator's love which is yours to use as you choose.

Lord Maitreya

The Christt Consciousness

Greetings, beloved ones. I am called the Lord Maitreya but I am also known as The Christ. I am the embodiment of the Christ energies for your planet.

The Christ energy represents that part of you which responds to the love of the Creator and, in turn, shares the Creator's love with all that is around you. You are created from the Christ essence, the love of Source. You are an expression of Its love and Its desire to expand Itself throughout space and time as It has formed it.

Your purpose is to love, to create love and to create through love. Love is the ultimate substance of everything around you: the light, the air, your physical Earth, and your physical bodies. They are all an expression of the love of the Creator. It is your task on the Earth to realize this, and to use this knowledge to expand what has already been done through your own creative effort. The love of the Creator is what keeps this expanding creativity within the limits of a specific Plan, which has purpose and meaning and serves all of those who exist within it.

By aligning your creative flow with the flow of love from the Creator, you assure that what you create will also serve the Creator's purposes. This is why we call ourselves cocreators. I include myself and you, also, in that category. We share the resources of Source Itself, as the Creator, to become cocreators with It. We are the ones who are responsible for creating the universe in which we live. Source has asked us to serve as cocreators with It to work out our purposes from the beginning, throughout the whole evolvement of those purposes.

My purpose is to serve as a focus for that creative flow within you which expresses the love of the Creator. It's my job to help all of you recognize that and to bring more of that creative flow into yourselves, and to express it more completely on the Earth. In your New Testament, I said, " All that I am and all that I do will be yours to do later, when you are able to express the Creator's will through your being." You can do more because you are working within the foundation which has already been laid by myself and those who have gone before you in physical existence. On the Earth, you will be greater creators, ever growing and evolving in your creative power.

Of course, there are many other spiritual beings here who are helping you evolve your cocreative abilities on the Earth. My particular focus within this Plan is to help you align with the creative love flow of the Creator. Then you can function with your heart as a guide and assure yourselves that through that connection you create what the Creator wants to create on Earth. That does not mean you do not have any impact on what is created. You are allowed to interpret this Plan according to your own strengths and abilities, to make your own unique contribution to this Plan for the Earth's evolution. The love focus that I bring allows you to see that your heart chooses to align to the Creator's flow and chooses to cocreate with his Plan for the Earth.

I have spent many lifetimes on the Earth. I was the first Earth human to achieve a full soul consciousness while within physical existence. Some of you had done this before me and have done it since, but you did it with the knowledge you had gained on other planets. I used only what I had learned from the Earth itself. This does not mean that I have more potential than you. It simply means that I, at that time, was a special focus for the creative flow of Source as it was being expressed on the Earth. After that lifetime, I moved to the spiritual plane and did not feel that it was necessary for me to work within physical existence anymore. I have since then been expanding my understanding of this creative love flow from the Source by studying the way it works on many other planets throughout this galaxy and this universe.

I am really an aspect of a Christ consciousness which is universal, and exists within every civilization in the universe. Each planetary experience has its own expression of the Christ consciousness, an aspect of the whole Christ consciousness which brings the creative flow of the Creator to that planet. It allows all of those there to have a focus which helps them align with the love of Source and enables them to express it through their own hearts.

I can recall one lifetime on the Earth in particular, when I explored what love meant. I wandered for many years as an orphan, growing up and maturing because of the generosity of all those individuals with whom I came in contact. I was fed by those whom I asked and clothed and sheltered by them when necessary. In return I was able to share with them some of the love that was within me. As a result, they always felt they had gained more by sharing with me than they had given.

I suppose I became something of a legend at that time, because I was a child who wandered from one place to another. Those with whom I came in contact were never sure where I would turn up or how long I would stay. I feel that, in that lifetime, I was being guided by the Source flow of love within me to share that love with all who chose to receive it. I think I gave them an opportunity to express this love by showing kindness to me. I think they were able to show more kindness to others after that because of what they had learned through their connection with me. I did not live a long lifetime then. At about the age of 27, I went out to sea in a boat one day and simply became light and returned to a spiritual level.

However, that was not my last physical lifetime. I spent some time in the higher dimensions; and some time at the university on Sirius, researching certain aspects of physical existence and how it relates to the creative flow of Source, and how this Source flow could be anchored within physical existence. I then came back for a series of lifetimes on the Earth that were very strenuous and entailed much hard work, but from which I again learned a great deal.

I tell this story because so many of you who are working to bring light to the Earth have done the same thing. You have reached the point of spiritual awareness that would allow you to leave physical existence yet you have chosen to return to help the Earth anchor more of the spiritual light within itself, and to help humanity realize its full cocreative abilities as a part of Source Itself and as an expression of Source love.

I would like to share my experiences and my learning with the Earth. I would like to share with you the focus of love which I am bringing to the Earth from this spiritual viewpoint. You can attune to me at any time. Many of you know how to do this. Some of you are still a little afraid that you are not worthy of receiving my love. This is a misperception which is within you and certainly is a feeling that I do not share. I offer myself to you at any time. Perhaps, you could imagine me standing before you, handing you a bright silvery blue star. You can place that silver and blue star within your heart as an expression of my love which is available for you to use on the Earth as a part of your life. I would like to help you understand more of what love can do and more of what love can create. I want to help you in your efforts to serve the Earth and to bring more light to her. Through using my energies, you will be able to do this for yourselves as well as for your Earth.

Thank you for this opportunity to share with you. I hope I will have many more opportunities like this, as you learn to go within yourselves and take advantage of the many wonderful learning opportunities that are available there for you in your own heart.

Exercise/Meditation

Imagine me as the sun god you once worshiped in Egypt or anyplace else. I can come through any form you choose to use if you are seeking a true connection to me. Imagine that I am standing in front of you. Let your imagination show you the form and the surroundings — a temple, a mountain top, even a ship travelling to the sun. Try to create surroundings that are designed to support your connection with me, for that is ideally what religion is all about. In this setting you and I are what is real; the surroundings are there to enhance our connection.

As you gaze on me, imagine that my light reaches out to you from my heart. Feel the light surrounding you and holding you secure and safe. Know that nothing from outside yourself can touch you now except love, because that is what I am. I am not judging you or expecting anything from you. I am simply responding to what you ask for. I want you to feel the love that I have for you. I know who you are and what your purpose is and I want to help you understand also. Your purpose is love, you are love. Allow my love to flow through you and help you understand that. Try to open yourself to me so that I can flow my love through you. You might feel a heaviness or even a slight pain somewhere as you do this, indicating an area of yourself that is afraid of my power or feels awkward in my light. Try to allow that area to fill with light, to radiate and expand as it releases its resistance to my flow.

As you become more comfortable with my energy, just relax into it and allow it to flow without any effort on your part except the desire to let it flow. I will flow into any part that I feel will be helpful to you. It will not always be the same place. Sometimes it will just be feelings of tension followed by release. Your mind might seem to wander to some problem. If you allow me to share it, I can help you solve it. I might be able to show you a clear picture of some past life that will help you understand how the problem began. I might be able to show you the next step.

The most important thing I would like to show you is what it feels like to love unlimitedly, what it is like to be centered in love. That is what you really are. I want to help you discover your own truth, your inner self, as love. If you can learn to allow my love to radiate from your heart, you can learn to allow your own divine self to be a part of you as a physical being on Earth.

I would love to practice flowing love with you any time, as often as you choose. If this practice brings up feelings of hopelessness or pain and anger at self, that's O.K. The light will bring up what you need to work on and I will be glad to help you release any negative feelings that come up as you work with me. The more negative feelings you recognize and release, the more room there will be for love in your light structure and the brighter it will shine. I am here to bring light to Earth and to physical existence just as you are. I want to work with you by helping you polish your light body. It's hard work but so much fun when the result is more light to share with Earth and the universe. That brings me so much joy that my light expands also.

Close your time with me with an affirmation that you are light and that love is the focus of your presence here.

Helios

A Life of Unlimited Joy and Love

I bring greetings to you all, my dear children. I am the consciousness that embodies your solar system. The sun is the center of my being, my heart. I have a great deal of love for each and every one of you. Each one of you is very special to me, and I seek, constantly, to share my light and my life force with you. My love is the core of that life flow which is ever coming to you. It is there for you if you will open yourselves to it, and allow that light to come into your heart to illuminate what you are and to illuminate the divine being that is within you.

I have watched your Earth grow and evolve for a long time. I have watched all of you growing and evolving with her. I am seeking to help you move more easily through these times, which will allow for the greatest movement forward your Earth has ever known and that you, as a part of the Earth, have ever experienced. I wish to let you know that my energies, my love, and my support are available to each one of you, and that you can always attune to me and ask for my help. If you need energy, I will give it to you. If you need healing and are ready to receive it, I can bring it to you. If you need support and understanding of how to relate to your Earth, I would like to help you with that also.

Your Earth is one of my very beautiful children. I love her as dearly as I love each of you. I do not love her more than you, although she is much larger than you. She has a special place in my heart right now because of the great growth that she is experiencing, and because of the great love that she is wanting to share with all of her family. This includes you, the animals, the plants and the crystals. She is also seeking to share her love with her brothers and sisters, the other planets in the solar system, and her cousins who are beyond your solar system — all of the family which makes up your galaxy.

The light of your sun is supported by my love, but it is also a reflection of a greater love, a greater light which comes from the center of the galaxy. More and more, I am bringing that energy through to the Earth now as she finds her place within the cosmos. That is all very difficult to understand, isn't it? I don't want to seem too serious. I want to be able to share my joy with you, the joy of the sunlight as it reflects on the waters of your planet or the joy of a warm summer's day as you walk or play in the sun. My joy is in providing the light that you use to evolve and be happy.

In times past, in your history, men have actually worshiped me and built temples to me. That was good because it helped them to understand a little bit more about what was beyond themselves and how their universe was constructed. I do not expect that from you. I ask that if you want to build a temple for me at all, build it within your hearts so that I can come in there and dwell as the radiant light of your own soul which is a greater expression of what you are now on the Earth.

The next step for humanity is to be able to dwell on Earth in full knowledge of itself as a group of divine beings, and in full harmony with its own soul and its soul's purpose. I would like to help you to attain that goal by helping you to focus within yourselves the light and the love that you need to accomplish this. Your Earth is seeking to achieve the same blending of her awareness with her divine consciousness, and of her soul, and as each of you attains this goal you aid the Earth in attaining hers.

When enough of you have become acquainted with your soul and have allowed it to become a part of your life, the New Age on your Earth can truly begin. You will enter into that period of experience on Earth that will provide you with more joy and satisfaction in your earthly experiencing than has been felt on Earth for a very, very long time. You will learn to do this in full conscious awareness of your divine beingness, your connection into the spiritual kingdom and your connection with your Creator, Itself.

When you think of me, imagine a warm, loving feeling within your heart that will be radiant and life-giving, healing and joyous, one that you can share with all of those around you and with your Earth itself. That is how I would like to be experienced on your planet now, as a part of yourselves which is divine, which is unlimited, which is loving and joyous and full of life.

Meditation/Exercise

Let's assume for this exercise that you are part of a group whether you have actually found a compatible group on Earth or not. Imagine that there are actual lines of energy going from the center of your heart which operates only at a level of absolute truth. Nothing negative or in opposition to your highest truth can exist here. If this is a new idea to you, that there is something in you that is absolutely true and good, just sit and enjoy that knowledge for a few minutes. The more you trust it, the more you can use it in your life.

Now imagine or feel that love energy from your heart center is moving from you along energy lines that connect you to your group. Your heart has an infinite supply of love in it so you will only increase the love available to you as you allow it to flow to your group. You might picture your heart center as a rose which radiates light, of whichever color feels good to you. And imagine the hearts of others as the other colors of the spectrum so that your group contains all colors within it. As the light flows through your spiritual connections to each other, you can feel their love blending with yours. The blending makes each one's light brighter and bigger. Their light supports you as you support theirs. Your individuality is enhanced rather than diminished by this sharing because your uniqueness is an absolute truth that is enhanced by using love. The more you share who you are and your creativity, the more you become the real you, unique and absolutely important to the Divine Plan.

You belong to many groups. Each aspect of your developing creativity has its own network. At some level every contact you make with another has a degree of importance in the whole picture of your life. Follow some of the lines which connect you to others in your group. You might be aware of a person that you know at the other end. You might just feel some quality of support that comes from them. You might feel that you are working out some difficulty in your relationship to this person. Since you are viewing this through your heart center, you can see the rightness of the viewpoint of each of you. From this perspective you can even see the solution, if not now, eventually.

You may eventually notice that not all the beings in your groups are in physical existence on Earth. Some are spiritual teachers, those in this book for instance. Your Master Kuthumi is an honorary member of every group as is your Christ, Lord Maitreya. They don't run the group or even tell you what to do, but they are available for advice and support where appropriate. Some of your groups may contain beings from many other places in this universe or others. Some may be struggling cocreators like yourselves, others may be quite cosmic in their awareness. But you are all equals and each has an equal say in what the group does.

You may notice that the group you attune to will be the appropriate one to help you with the problem or question of the moment. Some will feel close very often; others, rarely. If you can see an identifiable form, fine, but don't depend on it. Many of those in other dimensions who are working with you do not have physical forms. I don't. Many of the teachers in your Planetary Hierarchy do not use physical forms. We exist as light, of varying vibrational frequencies. But we are real and we are aware of your light.

You can explore your groups in any way you like. You can simply use the lines of light to support your love or you can develop friendships based on light connections. The point is to begin to trust that there are others who have the same light focus that you do, who are here to serve on Earth with love, and who are ready to work with you and support what you do.

Adonis

Becoming Aware of
the Creator within You

Dearest ones, I bring you love. I do not know how to convey in the English language all that love means to me and all of the potentialities of that word. What I want to convey to you is the recognition I see within each of you of the creative love growing, blooming and radiating from you in a way that is illuminating your Earth, and moving it forward in a direction that it has not been able to move before.

Your Earth is reaching a point where it is pulling together the many parts of itself which have been torn apart and scattered for so long. These are the parts of itself that work together to create a feeling of oneness and peace within. This feeling offers utter security in the knowledge of its place within the heart of the Creator. I see that integration now and I see its growing reflection in each of you. I see it producing a radiance and a growth of light within you that is bringing all of you, as a part of the Earth, together into a united expression that is love.

It brings you together because you want to work together, and because you love others enough to want to serve them as they represent the Source within. I have had many lifetimes at the physical level in other universes and times prior to this. I spent 2,600 lifetimes on one particular planet solving the problems of my own relationship to the light within and learning to allow it to shine forth and to be what I am, just as you are now doing.

There I learned to recognize that I was a part of the Creator, and that I was not separated because I was in a physical body. I was then able to move forward and take greater responsibilities within the creative effort. I became a member, and then a leader, of a large group that was spiritually supporting the evolution of a particular planet, at a crucial time. This planet was in the process of rebuilding its civilization — economic, social and religious structure — into one that would represent a unity of effort. Each one was learning to do his part of the whole, and each one was serving the whole rather than him or herself. This is a process of utilizing the strengths developed as an individual in the service of the whole and offering all of those strengths to be a part of the whole rather than keeping them for one's self and for one's own benefit.

The lesson that this planet learned was that nothing was lost in sharing strengths and in giving them to the whole and that there was gain by each from the strengths of the whole. They found they did not gain the strengths of the whole until they had completely given of themselves and their strengths to the whole.

The group I was working with was sending light energy to that planet, and guiding them to connect with this light so it could help them. To put it simply, as a group, we focused the thought form of the next step for the planet so they would have a framework on which to build and to guide themselves. This mental thought form was an energy framework of radiant light which could support or feed the energy requirements of those who could align with it and utilize it. It was the directing force and also the supply line for those who chose to work within it.

At first, only a few aligned with that mental thought form, but then over the years more and more began to. Finally every being within that planetary experience had learned to align with this flow of the ideal and, as a result, this ideal was manifested on their planet very clearly. From this experience I came to your universe, to your galaxy, and took a position which you might call "The Keeper of the Christ Light within each one." This does not mean that I hold it for myself, but that I hold the ideal of understanding that each of you is a creative point for Source, representing the will and the desire of Source to be creative and to experience at many levels within its creation. I have been holding this position since about the time your Earth was born. I focus the knowledge of its innate Sourceness, and also support the framework which binds each of you as "Bringers of Light and Love and Knowledge" into your creative effort on the Earth.

You could say that I am the knowledge of the divine light within each one of you that is seeking to come forth, to grow, to evolve and to create. I am the energy of ideal alignment into the Creator's Plan, which allows you to trust your connection and to use it with the assurance that it will lead you into the right use of your strengths and into the ideal completion of the Plan for your Earth. I am seeking to focus the divine light within you into a radiance that is creative and aligned into the flow of the Plan.

I am not the center point within you. I am the awareness of that center point and the flow of Source which comes from within that center point. Each of you is a center for the creative efforts of Source, a radiant point that generates light in accordance with the Plan and moves in alignment with it. The energy I focus helps you to understand what that means and helps you to evolve that into a creative expression as you work at your chosen position within the Plan.

The energy that I am flowing through this center point helps you to connect into the Plan, particularly now as it involves connecting into the center point of all of those with whom you work. Then you can become a group which is a center point for working out the Plan. You can share your strengths and your knowledge of your own Sourceness with the group. Together you can focus the love and the light and the knowledge from within out into the expansion of the creative effort.

I have been working with your Christ for many eons to aid Him in what He is doing for your Earth and to help Him bring this concept to you. He has been focusing love-wisdom for your Earth for you, but now it is time for you to work with Him and learn to do it for yourselves. He has great faith in the ability of humanity to love one another, to share and to work and grow as a group rather than as individuals. This is the thought form he has been projecting to the Earth for so long. It is beginning to take form more visibly now.

As more of you become consciously aware of the creative power of love-wisdom, and are able to translate it into useful action in your lives, you are able to expand beyond that and use the galactic perspective which I offer. This perspective allows you to serve as a group, not only for the Earth, but for the universe as well. This is the perspective that allows you to see that you are creators working toward a universal goal rather than an Earth-centered goal or an individual goal. You are not working toward your own individual evolution now. You are working for the evolution of the whole, because as a part of the whole you cannot evolve until the whole has progressed to the point to which you seek to bring it.

Those who are interested only in individual efforts rather than group efforts are leaving the Earth, and there will be few of them remaining after one hundred years have passed. Those remaining now are choosing to serve the purposes of the whole and learning to align their individual wills into the Higher Will and to serve there.

I would like to help you in this by offering you the support of my love and my energy as you align into this Higher Will with trust and a recognition that you are on the right path. I would like to use my energy to help you trust the group and its ability to serve the whole, and to trust yourselves to be able to find your place within the group. This trust then will lead to the validation of your efforts as you recognize that you are on the right path, that you have found the right group and that you are all working for the same purpose.

That is not as esoteric as it might sound. It is really quite scientific. What you are doing is aligning your own energy flow, the force of your own directed thought forms, with a stronger and more integrated thought form. That is being supported by creation itself and by the whole group of beings who are supporting the creative effort on the Earth. When you have aligned your thoughts with the flow of the more powerful or more divinely supported thought form of the Plan you are no longer battling to "swim up river." You are flowing with the full force of the mighty river of love which is flowing more and more strongly through your planet now. And like a mighty river, this flow draws into it everyone who seeks to come close and join with it. Eventually, it sweeps away everything in its path as it flows into the glorious conclusion of Source's Plan for creation.

You will find that you will not be lost in the mighty flow of this river, but that you will be sharing the true source of strength which is now yours within the universe. You will find that your individual purposes are not lost, but become a part of a whole which supports them absolutely and which manifests them ideally. You will find that you have not lost your individual identity, but have gained a greater identity which allows you to be more creative than you had ever thought possible. I would like to share this with you and be a part of the energy which is drawing you toward the path which leads to this mighty river, and which allows you to move into it comfortably and trustingly knowing that it is your ultimate purpose. As you move closer to becoming part of this flow, you begin to see that the creative source point within you is not small, limited, or hidden. It is something that grows and becomes more magnificent and powerful as it aligns with its fuller self which has not been confined within a physical body and truly is infinite in its expressiveness.

The Plan is love. It flows as light and it manifests as knowledge that you are love and light. Allow this flow of the Plan to become a part of your life in a way that allows you to evolve the light and love that is within you, and to drop any of the misperceptions and veils that hide them from you. Simply allowing yourself to feel that my energies and love will help you recognize that they are coming from within yourself as well as from without. It will help you to "water" that seed which is within so that it can grow, and so you can become a mighty cocreator of the Plan with your Earth and all of those beings who are a part of it.

My heart is with you and enfolds you. It is supporting you in every way that you accept. It trusts that you are manifesting a New Age of love, light and knowledge of your place within the love of Source now. I thank each one of you for sharing yourselves with me for this time.

Adonis.

Meditation

This is one of my favorite meditations. I am sitting in a large space on a throne. There are particles of light dancing all around me. I can project myself into these lights and they take me to new places. They show me many things and bring me back when I am done. Sometimes I go into more than one at a time. Sometimes I just dance with them. When I am done, I bring them all into myself and sit peacefully for a while. It makes me feel very complete.

Quan Yin

Focusing Joy for the Earth

Greetings, my friends. I am now a member of your Spiritual Hierarchy, but I spent many lifetimes on Earth. During my last life on the Earth I performed many acts of kindness. I was much remembered for this and was known for a long time as the Goddess Of Mercy. I am still seeking to promote that quality and helping to bring it to the Earth. I am also expanding my energies now to include the use of all of the heart qualities on Earth, especially to teach the Earth how to become more receptive to those qualities.

As a part of the physical Earth, you have the advantage of being able to learn within her. As you open your heart to kindness, to love, to joy, to peace and integrity, you allow the Earth and humanity to express those qualities with you and allow yourself to receive them also. This way you become a channel for these qualities.

You don't have to feel that you are particularly gifted in using these qualities, but I can assure you, if you allow yourself to be receptive to them and allow the teachers and the Earth to flow them through you in this way, they will become strengths because they are a part of what you already are. They are a part of that divinity within you that is perfect and already knows how to use the ideal flow that comes from the Creator Itself.

Using these qualities always feels difficult at first, because it seems the Earth does not receive them. That is one of the things I am working on. I am helping to suffuse the Earth with these energies so that it can receive them more easily. The key is to know that these energies are available to you, and that they can be a part of you which you can learn to express. Indeed, they are already within you and a part of yourself but you have not yet learned to use them completely. As you practice allowing these qualities to flow through you, you express them more easily and they become a part of yourself.

The Earth experience is a school, a training ground, in the use of your cocreator abilities. Being receptive to these Source qualities is part of the learning that you undergo on the Earth. You are not expected to do it all right the first time. What we do expect is that you continue to try to the best of your ability, to express these qualities that are buried in yourselves. We ask, simply, that you practice using them. With continual practice the perfection will come.

There will come a time when you can be a perfect channel for the love, the joy, the peace, the understanding, the clarity, and the truth that is available to you from the Source within you. When you learn to be the source of these divine qualities, you radiate them to others much more intensely than you would otherwise. You become an example for others to follow, just as the Master Jesus did when he allowed the Christ to work through Him. You become a part of the Earth that has learned to express itself in this way, as he did. Therefore, each step you take, each advance you make, is a victory for the Earth and a step in its growth. You are all searching for your spiritual purposes on the Earth. I would suggest that your common purpose is to help the Earth learn to express these divine Source qualities.

It doesn't have to be difficult. It is simply a process of looking for joy. Wherever you find it, allow yourself to feel joy and radiate it out again. Allow yourself to share every spark of joy that you find. Thus, you magnify it and in the sharing, it becomes a part of what you are and a part of what the Earth is. If you miss one spark of joy, you don't need to feel you've failed. You simply begin to look for the next one. Know that you will find it if you keep looking. Someone else will pick up that other spark and focus it for the Earth.

I've spent many lifetimes on the Earth learning to use these qualities myself. I spent one lifetime as what you might call a comic dancer, a kind of a juggler. My focus at that time was specifically to share joy. Before each performance, I would sit down, think of all the joyful experiences I could remember, and gather up all of the joy I could find within and around myself. I filled myself with joy and therefore found it easier to express it and share it through my dancing.

I would suggest that you might like to try the same thing. At the beginning of each day, think of everything you can that is joyful. You might make it your focus for a week. Make a list of things that are joyful, things that bring joy to you or that brought joy to others. Collect all of these, place them within your heart and seek to share joy with others for a week as "your heart quality emphasis" for that week. Make joy the focus of everything you share with others for that time.

The next week you can go on to a different quality of the heart. As you cycle through all of the various heart qualities that you feel you would like to perfect, you will want to repeat them after a time. I think, each time you go through the cycle, you will learn to express these qualities on a higher level and you will begin to see them affecting your life. You will see how they support one another and how they magnify their effects when they work together. I would like very much to help you with this. If you would like to focus my energies while you are collecting your heart qualities, I would be glad to help you do so. You can invoke me any time of the day that you need help. You can invoke me before you go to sleep at night if you feel that you would like to research ways to use joy and opportunities to bring more joy to the Earth. This will help the Earth learn to use this quality more than it has been able to before. The Earth has much joy, much love, much peace within it, just as you do. It's learning to express them as a divine being, just as you are.

You truly are partners with the Earth in learning to use your divine qualities. Throughout all of this, you will be learning to recognize these qualities within yourself, and to receive them from others. This is perhaps the most important thing of all to recognize; that everything is a part of Source and has already been placed within your heart for you to use and develop as divine creative beings. Your life on Earth is an especially good opportunity for you to use these in a sharing way with others as a member of a group, which is the Earth.

Thank you very much for this opportunity to speak with you about what I am doing. I really would like to work with many of you and share what I have learned about using these divine heart qualities here on the Earth.

My love to you. Quan Yin.

Meditation

Imagine you are standing on a seashore. The water is warm and invit-ing. It doesn't matter if you actually know how to swim or not; you know the water is your friend and you don't need to fear it. Out on the waves you can see us jumping and calling you. You feel our message carried to your heart on the wind. You realize that it is all right to dive in and join us so you do. Suddenly you are swimming with us in the sea, leaping out of the waves and diving deeply into the sea again and again, leaping out of the warm sea into the sparkle of spray and sunshine. In the water we are all close to you, sometimes our bodies touch to let you know that we love you.

One of us offers you a ride. You can sail along through the waves as you did long ago, perhaps in Atlantis. Leave your worries and cares behind you, wash them away in the sea. Let joy be your only thought. Joy is all that matters, joy of love for the sea, the Earth, for us your teachers in feeling joy. There is really no limit to the joy you can feel. We can help you go beyond physical existence to feel the joy that is in water, air and light. Let the joy flow through every cell of your being.

Know that your body allows you to feel joy through being physical also. It adds another dimension of joy to your existence that makes you deeper and more than you were. Allow this joy to radiate from all parts of yourself as light that makes the earth brighter. It's fun. Life can be fun if you stop struggling with yourself and Earth. Just leap from one experience to the next, not worrying what is going to happen. The light will make whatever happens a joyful experience if you just let it flow through you.

Imagine that life is a sea of love and joy that supports you at every moment of your life, bringing you endless opportunities to experience new things, to learn about yourself. Life on dry land may seem much more complicated that swimming in the sea, but maybe it doesn't have to be. Pretend that every new situation is one that you can sail through as if one of us were carrying you on our back. We can be your friends and companions in spirit, providing an aura of joy that permeates your life.

Merista (Dolphin)

A Message of Joy and Love

I am called Merista and I am a dolphin. That is the name that I use among my friends. I live in the Pacific Ocean, traveling many thousands of miles at times through the warmer waters there. I very much enjoy the opportunity to exist on this beautiful planet and experience the wonderful oceans that are available for us to swim in. I also enjoy leaping into the air and looking at the sun and the sky and the clouds, the atmosphere of this planet.

The sea itself, as you know, is a wonderful place with much life, many interesting plants and, for the most part, plenty of food. We live a life of little care and, save for the invasion of our domain by man, we have a very wonderful existence.

Many of you are concerned about the destruction of our race. We recognize that there are many of you who are working now to make life more secure for us, so that our race can continue on Earth. We are grateful for that. It is because of this support that is coming from some members of humanity that we are making an effort to stay. At one point we had decided that there was no reason to remain on the Earth and that we would allow ourselves to be destroyed. That has changed. We sense a growing awareness within humankind of the value of this beautiful Earth, and the value of a clean and balanced existence on the Earth for all species.

We see that it will be some time before it will be entirely safe for us to move freely within these waters. We are striving to remain so that when that time has passed that it is not safe for us, there will be enough of us left to continue our race on the Earth. Many of us still wish to remain here to experience and aid humanity in any way that we can. We love humanity very much, even though it has seemed that humanity was going to destroy us.

We understand your purposes on the Earth because, as you are light beings, so are we. We have been bringing light to this planet for many, many eons. We were once beings who walked on the dry land of the Earth and carried light to the Earth in that manner. When we had finished our experiencing and learned all that we could in that manner, we decided to move into the sea and continue bringing light into the Earth, leaving the dry land for humans to master.

Through this fluid medium in which we are working now, we find it easier to communicate with humanity and aid them by bringing light into the Earth. We are very eager to communicate with you so that we can share what we know of the Earth and light and of how to blend the two. We want to be able to share what we understand of the Creator and the creative potentials within each of us. We want to help the Earth and humanity develop its creativity as light beings aligned with the divine purpose. For this reason, some of us have allowed ourselves to be captured and live among humans, so we can be a reference point for our whole race. This allows a much closer contact than is possible otherwise. Those who are in captivity remain in contact with all of us through our inner awareness. They share what they learn of humanity, its goals and purposes, from that close association. At the same time, we are able to support them with our love and our spiritual connections, so that we can help sustain them in the rather limited space in which they are confined.

Our message to you is that Earth is a light and joyful place and there is much to experience here that is of a wondrous and exciting nature. If you would like to attune to our energies, imagine yourself moving through the waters of a warm and fertile ocean. You may be able to tune into some of our thoughts. You may be able to hear our song. You may be able to hear our communication with the Earth or with its divine Creator.

We would like to help you in our own way to make that divine connection with the Earth and with the Creator through your own consciousness. In this way, you can bring more light into the physical structure of the Earth and allow yourselves to exist more and more as light beings.

Ours is not a complicated message. It is one of joy and love, of a desire to serve and of a desire to love and be loved. We offer you our love in great abundance and invite you to come share love with us.

Thank you.

✧ Part V

PUTTING THE PLAN
INTO ACTION

Exercise

Imagine that I am sending you a blue flame. It comes into your heart and then into all your chakras. I can direct it through your heart to help you release anything that is not truth and love. You can use this blue flame to heal yourself, to assist others in healing themselves or to transform your environment and your life. Difficult problems may recur but if we keep working to banish them, they will improve and eventually disappear.

When you feel the area we are working on is clearer, use the blue flame to fill it with forgiveness, love, joy and peace. My blue flame is always available, whenever you seek it.

Archangel Michael

Finding Your Spiritual Center

I am Michael the Archangel, Guardian of the sixth level and Protector of the Center. I embody the Ideal, the sixth level, of the Plan. I am the guardian of that special spiritual divine place within yourself, that center point where you know absolutely that you are divine and that you are a part of the whole. When I say I am the protector, I mean that I recognize most clearly that this center spot within yourself can never be destroyed, can never be apart from what you are.

My energies serve as a bridge into this point for each one of you. This bridging is available to you at any time that you are ready. This means that as you reach into this point within yourself, you are seeking to activate all of your divine strengths and divine potential. You are certainly seeking to align with your soul's purpose and this center point is where you connect into your soul and your divine purpose. This center point is covered up or hidden by the misperceptions of many lifetimes of experiencing on the Earth where you did not see clearly that you were a part of Source and that you were divine.

I am the energy that you use to clear away these misperceptions, these veils which have hidden from you your true power. That's why I am called the Protector and Defender of the Just. I protect that which is most true within you and I aid you in aligning into it.

In order to utilize the strength of this great divine creative power within you, you must be clear in your whole vehicle. That means your body must be strong and healthy and aligned with the soul's purpose. Your emotions must be positive and you must be able to utilize the higher emotions such as love, joy, wisdom, peace. Your mental body must be free of fixations upon lesser goals, personality or material desires and be able to conceptualize an ideal.

As you clear your vehicle, each step allows you to become more balanced. You connect more clearly with the clarity of your soul through your center point. Sometimes I can help you to achieve a glimpse of this center point, which will give you a glimpse of the goal and serve as a guide for your forward movement.

As you attune to me, you might see before you a blue-white flame. Step into this energy and feel it clearing away all the resistance to knowing what you truly are as a divine being. This energy need not be hot. It can be cool and tingling and it can be very relaxing and peaceful if you will allow it. As you step into it, allow this energy to flow through you into the very center of your being. Feel it in the center of your heart. Feel it moving deeper and deeper into this center, reaching for the core of your divine being. As it reaches deeper into your heart, it becomes radiant and begins to shine outward. This outward movement can then carry away all resistance to the light so that more light can come in. As more comes in, more of the burden, density, and covering is lifted from your heart so that you can see it more clearly and use its energies in the ideal way.

If you hold this focus for as long as you can (even five minutes is very effective) and do it daily, it will help you to clear yourself. It will help you to see areas that need to be worked on within yourself. It will also prepare the way for more specific connections into your heart. What you will actually be doing is allowing your soul to make a connection through you into your purpose on the Earth. As these connections become clear, you will begin to connect into the Plan for the Earth and the framework of the Earth's forward movement, so that you become a part of that. Thus, you become a cocreator within it and are supported by it. Then you can work within it, knowing that what you do is appropriate, needed and a part of your purpose.

I am the substance of the balancing point between you and Source, which maintains not only the difference between you and Source, but also the unity between you and divine Source. Others of the archangels embody other levels of creative manifestation. My energy exists particularly as the central area, but it radiates out and interpenetrates all other layers forming a bridge from the most dense manifestation of physical existence to the highest, purest, truest light that is Source Itself.

I am not a "short cut" back to Source but a balancing or centering point which can allow you to experience all levels of Source's creation without becoming separated from it. As cocreators, you have chosen to go out from Source and experience the many levels of creativity that Source has provided. At the same time, Source has given you many balancing points and ways of remaining connected during this exploratory creative experience that you are going through.

It is necessary to experience creativity directly at its many levels of manifestation in order to master it and control it in the way that Source does. This will eventually make you a Creator in your own right. At the same time, Source has provided you with a link to Itself which allows you to remain a part of the whole while you experience and explore your own individual creative potential. I am here to help you see and remember that, while you are exploring your potential as an individual, you remain a part of Source. You are an aspect of Source's creativity. You experience for Source and It supports you in everything that you do. I have been serving in this way since your creative experience began, and I will continue to do so until the end.

I am the substance of the rock upon which Christ founded his church. It is that center point, that eternal Source Connection which is always there, open and available to you. The more each of you aligns with my energies and recognizes them and uses them, the stronger I become and the more my energies reach those who do not see them and attune to them so easily. When enough of you have recognized my presence within you and know how to use it as a foundation for your creating on the Earth, a critical mass will be formed which will align the whole of the Earth into that center point. I am looking forward to that event, planning for it and enlisting the help of all those who wish to help me achieve it. I am actively working to draw to myself, as this center point, all of the cocreators on the Earth, so that what they create will truly be aligned with what Source wishes for the Earth. In this way, your New Age will truly be an expression of what Source has always desired for the Earth — to make it a beautiful garden of love and light which allows each individual to explore their own creativity, and to expand and share it in a way that allows the whole to know itself more clearly.

I will not be diverted from my purpose. That is not my nature. You can trust me to always be there and to always be ready to reach out a hand to guide you, if you ask. You must learn to ask because we will not impose upon your free will or do anything that opposes it. I stand ready to help you cut the bonds of misperception that are limiting your realization of your full divine potential. I stand ready to guide you on the path that leads you to that center which is all that you are. I have great love for each one of you, and I make it available to you in every way that I can. I pray that you will learn to recognize it more and more and thus be able to utilize it for yourselves and for your Earth.

My gratitude to you for the time you have spent with me and for any time that you share with me in the future. My love goes out to you as the Creator's love being shared with you through me. Thank you.

Meditation

When you meditate or even when you go to sleep at night, try this so as to build a stronger connection with us. Imagine that there is a large tube of light coming from your ship or star. It comes around you from your left side, surrounds you and goes back up to its starting point. The energy flowing through this tube is healing and balancing. We can work through it to activate the necessary changes in your body and energy field. Holding a quartz crystal in each hand or placing four to six of them around you will help also. Sleeping in or under some sort of pyramid arrangement will work also, if you make the conscious decision to allow us to use its energy.

You may have sensations of energy moving around you or have dreams which indicate something unusual happened to you. We can work to heal your emotional flow as well as your body and we can help you deal with any difficult energy memories which arise as a result of what we do. You can stop this at any time by telling us to go away.

Zeewin

Teachers and Guides from Beyond Earth

I greet you with love in my heart for you and your Earth. I am a commander of one of the galactic fleets which is working with your Earth to aid her in establishing the New Age. The primary goal of the group with which I am working is to aid humanity in developing the strengths and qualities needed to create this New Age, and to live in it in a way that allows the Earth to express the highest potential that she can at this point.

I have had a few lifetimes on this Earth, one during the Lemurian times, one during the Atlantean times and one much earlier than either of those. These were not lives as a famous person nor were they difficult lives. During the Lemurian lifetime, I was involved in a war against beings from another planet who were trying to invade Earth and impose their ways upon you.

Part of what I am doing now with specific members of my group is to repair some of the damage done. During the Lemurian lifetime, I was a member of that alien race who had reincarnated into humanity and was seeking to aid in the resolution of the conflict. I was not one of those who was seeking to invade your Earth.

These beings from another planet had a particularly strong mental focus and were very adept at using mental energy. They were trying to bring this ability to your Earth. They saw that it was the next step for the Earth and that help was needed in developing it. What they did not see was that the Earth was not quite ready to take that step all at once. Some of the beings from this other planet saw only the goal and were not kind or gentle about the means of attaining it. They were overly zealous and tried to bring about the change too fast. Some were operating from pure selfishness. Some thought they were doing the right thing, but did not understand humanity enough to see they were not being received well.

My part during that lifetime on the Earth was spent as a leader. I worked with a particular group of humans, as an emissary to the alien beings, who tried to resolve the differences and help to persuade them that their course of action was not the right one for the Earth. My purpose was not that easily achieved and it took another 150 years before the war was finally ended.

All in all, the war lasted 500 years and left a lasting impression on humanity. This is a deeply buried memory, one that humanity has not dealt with for a long, long time. Now, as your contact with aliens on this planet grows, it is bringing up these memories from your subconscious. It is something with which you have to deal if you are going to learn to work cooperatively and productively with beings from other planets who are interested in helping you now.

Your Earth has reached the point where she should be able to work with beings from other planets and with other energies that are unfamiliar. She must be able to allow them to help her see the details of the next step and what she must do to move forward. She is learning to do this without invoking interference from others which is not appropriate and which is detrimental to the welfare of her kingdoms, humanity and herself.

That long war, of which I spoke, is past and the beings who were involved in it have seen that was not the way to accomplish their purpose. They have paid, all of them, karmically for the harm which they caused your Earth. They are here now not only to repay the damage that was done, but to cooperate with the Divine Plan and to use it to aid and to guide them as they work with you now.

The doorways of Earth have been closed to those who come without the acceptance of humanity. Anyone who comes now must be invited by someone or some group on the Earth. It is up to humanity to choose with whom they wish to work. If there are beings from outside Earth on your planet who are not serving the good of the whole, know that there is another group on Earth who has invited them and who has decided to work with them. When enough of the whole of humanity clearly understands what kind of help they want, and what influences they want to bring to the Earth from other worlds and other galaxies, the will of the whole will prevail and there will no longer be those who form conspiracies or partnerships to work for the gain of only a few.

Another part of our purpose now is to help humanity connect into the Plan, to the goal, to use the help that is available. We can also guide them to choose with knowledge and understanding the path that they take. In this way, they can choose their own destiny and be in control of their own progress.

Our job now is not to come directly onto the Earth and be among you at the physical level. We are working from the spiritual levels. We do not have third-dimensional physical bodies at present. We exist primarily in the fifth, sixth and seventh dimensions and we work from there. We are helping you to clear your mind and your emotional bodies so you can communicate with us and receive the help we have to offer.

The important focus right now is for each of you to become clear channels for your own higher selves, so that connection can bring you the help you need from other dimensions. We work with individuals and groups upon your Earth to instill new ideas for clearing your subconscious and for balancing the energies within your mental, emotional and physical bodies. We also have the technical means to aid in rebuilding your etheric structures, and helping you rebuild the connections into the higher aspects of yourself.

Each one of you has a specific ship or group who works with you. We do much of our work through a process you know as radionics and your ship has an energy blueprint for each of you in our computers. They look at your light and the way you are using energy now and determine what the next step is for you. Then, they focus their energies through certain crystal apparatus which surrounds you with the next level of energy to be used or the corrections for the energy flow that you are using now. This serves as a guide with which you can align. Then, step by step you can move into a more ideal use of the energy potential that is available to you.

We are not forcing you into any structure which we have conceived, but helping you achieve the ideal which you have set for yourselves. We look at your goals and your place in the Plan and then help you align into your purpose more clearly. This is a means of speeding up your evolution, and it is an aid which is going to help you achieve your purposes faster than you would otherwise.

When you release some block in one part of your body, for instance, it may leave a lot of "loose ends" in your aura which need to be cleaned out. Normally, they would dissipate with time, since they are no longer being nurtured by the core which has been released. We help you clear that out much more rapidly, so you are ready for the next realization or the next clearing procedure. We are also working a great deal with balancing the mental and emotional bodies, and we can help you see how to use each of these energy levels within yourself so they work harmoniously together rather than in opposition to each other. If you visualize a connection to us and consciously utilize our energies, you help to bypass any subconscious resistance you have to allowing another individual to work on your body. If you can learn to trust us and allow this conscious attunement, you will be aided much more by the spiritual help which we have to give.

Much of the work being done already on your Earth by innovative psychologists, healers, and counselors has been inspired by us. Most of you are friends and have previous connections with those of us who are here now. You recognize us on another level and are willing to work to help us help you move ahead. You are working with old friends, not strangers, who are here to help you. We are not more spiritual than you. We are not any wiser than you. We are simply focused at another level which sees a little more clearly and from a broader perspective, so we can give you the benefit of this way of looking at yourself and your next step.

As you reach a clearer alignment of your four bodies, your physical, mental, emotional and spiritual bodies, you begin to clear away the subconscious limitations that are keeping you from seeing your full potential. As you allow yourselves to be the divine light that you are, you will reach a level of balance within yourself that is much more connected into your higher dimensional levels. At this point, there are those of us who will help you to learn to use these higher dimensions, to master them and to bring a broader perspective of understanding of your potential into the physical plane.

I am talking here about learning to utilize such inherent abilities as transporting yourself to any part of the Earth or the Earthly environs that you wish. You also have the potential to see clearly at any distance and to see into the past and sometimes into the future. Another useful ability is to move freely from one dimension into another and return to the physical. The abilities to shape matter mentally, to manifest from the mental/spiritual perspective into the physical plane, to communicate telepathically, to attune very clearly and directly to the spiritual teachers at many levels are also available to you. These are only a few of the abilities that humanity will be developing in the next one thousand years. Some of them are beginning to be used on your Earth now, and more of them will be available in the next few hundred years.

All of these abilities involve profound changes within the structure of the four-body system. We can help you to stabilize that and to keep a clear perspective as you move into the use of these higher powers. We will help only those who have spiritual intentions. The development of these skills will be much more difficult for those who intend to use their new abilities selfishly and for wrongly directed aims. This is not only by our choice, but simply because of the nature of the energy connections which are made through your right desires and bring you the help that is appropriate.

I would be very happy to talk with any of you who wish to work with me, to help you to determine the next step for your own development and to put you in touch with those who will be specifically appropriate for you to work with. I have a large staff which is available to work with any of you, at any time that you wish. If you attune to me, you may not connect with me directly, but you will get someone within my group who is working with the Plan, and who is a part of a group energy that has access to the information and the resources that you need.

Many of you are aware of your own ship or your own particular space friends. Generally, these are individuals who are working with you and are already doing much of what I have described. It is beneficial for you to work consciously with them and utilize them whenever possible. To attune to us, you simply need to visualize a ship overhead which is directing a beam of energy down to you. Send a beam of energy from your heart to the ship and then feel the response. Allow this response to flow through you into the Earth and back up through you, so you are anchored into the Earth and you are aware of the support the Earth has for what you are doing.

This also connects you into the rest of the group that is humanity so that your learning can be shared with, and supported by, the rest of humanity. Initially, if you can simply envision this connection, that is all that will be necessary. Only five minutes is effective. If you do it before you go to sleep, it will allow a smoother transition into those work areas where we can help you on the Inner Planes while you are sleeping. If you see an image or hear a name or get a message, that is helpful but not necessary.

Keep some kind of record of what you receive. You can validate the truth of what you have received by its effect on you. I do not recommend that you take at face value everything that you receive initially until you have learned whether or not it can be trusted, and whether or not you are receiving it accurately. I say this because sometimes the mind, in its desire to make the contact, will create a fantasy of what it thinks is occurring. You know this is happening when this fantasy does not provide you with any concrete results. If an actual contact has been made, you will feel results in a sense of peace, perhaps a sense of renewed purpose, or better yet, some ideas you need to use yourself or to help you to work with others more clearly and more productively.

There is much growth going on in your Earth. Much progress is being made and we are very happy to see that. We are glad to help in any way that we can. Know that we are here to serve you, not ourselves, and that we are here to serve together within the Plan to create a New Age on your Earth which will make her a light for the whole galaxy, for the whole universe. We seek to bring light and we can support you as light bearers on the Earth.

My love to you and my sincerest wishes for peace and happiness and love for your Earth. Thank you.

Exercise

Listen to some nice, sparkly music while you do this. Imagine that you are standing on a surface of white light. In front of you is a large, broad stairway. The first step is red light, the second is orange and so on through yellow, green, blue and violet. Practice climbing the staircase, stopping on each step to absorb and integrate the energy. When you reach the top, you can dance up and down the steps however you like. I will be there to dance with you. You can extend the staircase upward so that the spectrum repeats endlessly and you and I dance all over it. You are always receiving new energy from each level.

At some point you will be able to jump off the stairway onto one of the many light beams which extend in all directions around it at all angles. Dance from one to the other. There will be others dancing with you. Sometimes the light beams carry you far out and bring you back. Sometimes they stop and let you off on another light beam. It's fun. I like doing this. When you are done, climb back down the original steps and rest on your white light.

Celestial Light (An Angel)

Help in Using Your Full Light Potential

Greetings. I bring you my love. I call myself Celestial Light, because I am an aspect of light which is brighter than what you have been accustomed to seeing and using. It is my purpose to help you to stretch into this finer and more intense light now available to you.

Your Earth has been evolving rapidly in the past few years and is learning to use new frequencies of light. Each time she reaches a new level of understanding of her divine potential, she draws more light to herself. This new light is not only brighter and of a higher frequency, but it is also more electrical and produces a great deal more activity in your body.

Some of you are having difficulty now assimilating this light within your physical and emotional structures. So, I have been invited by Vywamus to join the group in this book. He is concerned that many of you are having trouble using this light, which is such a potent aid for you now in moving into those higher levels of spiritual understanding. I am an angelic being — one of many who are embodying the new level of electromagnetic energy that is coming to the Earth now. Part of my job is to aid you in connecting into these rays and helping you to use more of this potential that is available to you now. I feel very happy about the amount of light that you have invoked, and certainly about the amount of light that you on Earth have accepted. However, we see some blocks within you that prevent your full usage of the potential of this light and which make the movement forward more difficult.

Vywamus has been working particularly in helping humanity to clear the mass consciousness and to clear their own subconscious structures, so they can see more clearly the potential use of this light within themselves. They, then, can release the fear of using this high energy source. He has asked me to make myself known and to offer you the opportunity to connect into my energies which can help you adapt to and utilize this new level of light within yourself.

Each vibrational level of light has its own particular framework for development. When the Earth was very, very young, the light which the Earth received allowed for the initial formation of physical bodies of humanity. Later, as the vibrational level rose and the light shifted, the consciousness of man began to appear. With another shift in light, man developed the ability to connect unconsciously with his feelings and emotions. More recently in the history of the Earth, another light shift caused man to become more mentally active which began the great surge of scientific advancement which is now moving forward on your planet, and which is moving you into many areas with which you need to learn to deal as cocreators with your Earth. This level of light which is coming in now step by step will allow humanity to recognize their own spiritual potential and help them to recognize themselves as divine beings. This light can help them see that they can be cocreators of an Earth that will support them and allow them to live in harmony and peace with one another and with the other species of life on the Earth.

The Earth itself has a potential for infinite abundance and for supporting all forms of life, whether they be plant, animal or human. It can allow each to use his or her fullest potential as a divine being, working with a Supreme Creative Source. Within this new conscious awareness is the potentiality for developing a group awareness which takes into account the needs of the whole, rather than the needs of the few or one individual. This is a higher awareness which allows you to experience, creatively, your oneness with "All That Is." At the same time, you learn to work with others in creating a physical environment which reflects that oneness and a desire to express the infinitely abundant potentials of the Earth for all.

Stretch your minds past the anxiety of providing for your own needs and the fear that there is no place for you on the Earth. Imagine this infinite abundance as evenly distributed across the Earth, so that each one can live as he wishes. See that each one is a part of the creative effort which is the Earth. Feel the peace and the contentment which comes with knowing that you will never lack what you need. Feel the confidence that will arise within your own self as you realize that there is an opportunity to move forward to the highest level of your creative potential without limiting others in their achievements. Feel that group awareness which allows you to share the forward movement of another and which allows them to share your forward movement. See how, as each of you moves forward as an individual, you allow yourself to move with the group, and be aided by the group as you aid the group.

Those who cannot envision this in some way within themselves will not remain on the Earth much longer, because the Earth has moved past the point where it will provide a home for individual interests. It is time for the development of group interests. Those who have not seen the limiting effect of selfish creation will be moved to another place which provides them with the opportunity to evolve their creative potential in the way, and at the speed, they choose.

Those of you who are ready to move creatively as a group, who wish to live harmoniously with the Earth and all of her kingdoms, and who wish to explore more and more of your divine potential as spiritual beings, are the ones who are preparing now to create a new Earth and a New Age. In order to make room for the new level of light awareness within yourself, you must let go of the old awareness. You must let go of your feelings of limitation and your desire to remain at the same level simply because it is comfortable and familiar. You must release the fear of moving into "unknown territory" and learn to trust that the flow of the light will gradually carry you into higher and higher dimensions of your own consciousness. Then you can recognize and utilize the powers that are within you.

You do not need to do this all at once. You can do it step by step. When you feel some growth within you, you must be willing to let go of what is no longer needed;or it will build up a blockage and resistance within you, which limits the flow of light and help that you get from allowing this light to flow through you.   You must consistently study yourselves and look deeply within to find what you need to release. If it is a fear, then this fear must be replaced by trust that you are light, as light cannot be destroyed and will provide for your needs. If it is hate for anyone or anything, this must be replaced by unlimited love that flows through you from the Creator. If there are feelings of loss or feelings that Earth cannot provide for you as a spiritual being, these must be replaced with a confident awareness of the infinite abundance which is available to you through the Earth. Allow yourself to see it and to receive it. The list of things to be released is different for each individual but, in general, they are quite similar for all.

There are many aids available to you now if you wish to clear yourselves and allow this new awareness of your creative abilities to come forth. When you have truly released your misperceptions of lack of abundance or your limitedness and inability to move as light on the Earth, you will find that you are able to do things which appear impossible or miraculous. When you recognize your own unlimitedness, you will be able to be anywhere you wish at any time. You will be able to have anything you desire. You will be able to move to any level of awareness and bring that awareness to the Earth. You will be able to experience finer and finer levels of spiritual awareness and bring them into the physical plane. You will recognize that spiritual awareness is something that belongs within the physical, and that it can blend with it and move with it now!

All of you are attuning to this spiritual light now more and more clearly, each in your own way, and seeing within it the Plan for this New Age. The inspirations and the ideas you receive for building a better planet are coming to you on this light. They are being focused within the light by divine beings who work with the Earth and aid her in her evolution. They provide their spiritual awareness and their higher interpretation of the Divine Plan, and focus it into the Earth at a level which is easier for you to receive. By allowing this light to become a part of you and to flow through you, you avail yourself of the higher energies which will move your body into a higher energy state or a higher awareness. It can also bring you the creative ideas and the knowledge that you need to create this New Age on the Earth.

To utilize this higher energy state and to utilize the help that I bring in accepting this new energy, imagine yourself surrounded by a field of iridescent light that is constantly flowing from every direction to you and through you. This light is loving and supportive and understands the level at which you are working now. It will come in to the extent that you can allow it to move you forward and become a part of you.

When I say this light becomes a part of you, I do not mean that it becomes a static thing within you. You need to learn to visualize the light as a constant flow. It is a continual receiving and giving, a moving forward and letting go of what is no longer needed. Accepting this light implies that you are becoming a part of the divine flow, which will support you and move you forward, providing you with a secure foothold in your own awareness of yourself as a creative being.

This new light is the next step in understanding more of the potential for infinite creativity and growth for you and the Earth. Allow me and the others who are represented in this book to serve you as we aid you in learning to utilize this light and to move into these greater and more cosmic potentialities.

My love for you is great. I do not look at what you perceive as limitation or lack; I see only your potential. I recognize your light and seek to help you to become more light, and to use more of what is available for you within the light. As you accept each new level of light, the next level will become available to you and you will have the support that you need to move into it.

Thank you for your love, for your desire to serve and for your desire to move forward and evolve. That is truly what life and consciousness are about: continual growth and evolving an understanding of what you are.

Meditation

Imagine a bright star overhead. There is much love coming to you from this star. When you can feel the love or know that it is there, allow it to come down into your heart. Now feel the love flowing from your heart. Let it fill your body and energy field. Then let it flow from your eyes, hands and feet. Just let it flow for a while.

Practice this with a partner also. Look at him or her with all this love flowing from your eyes. Do they look different? Hold your hands over some area of the body which needs healing and let the love flow. This is the ultimate healing tool. During any task, let the love flow from your feet. Do things feel or work out differently now?

Korton

Using Love in Communication

G reetings to you, my dearest friends. I am a member of the Space Command. I exist in the sixth-dimensional form, but I am, I think, very much a part of your physical experience on Earth, and very much interested in everything that's going on on the Earth now. I have worked with the Earth for many, many eons. I have been here as long as Ashtar and we have worked together for that length of time. We share the same hopes and the same love for the Earth. I have the deepest respect and gratitude for Commander Ashtar, and for what he has done and is doing for the Earth. I endeavor to assist him in any way that I can.

My particular area of expertise is communications, and I would like to talk about that with you. I am not necessarily referring to the physical setup of radio sets and receivers tied together by computers which allows us to communicate. That is very much present within the Space Command, and I am the coordinator of that. There is much, much more to communication than that. Actually, very little of the actual communication at the organizational level of the Space Command is carried out using actual physical equipment.

Most of our work is done through a clear perception of the Plan of the Commander which is received intuitively by us. There is a "meeting of minds" which allows us to share our thinking and to let each know how we feel about things. We can attune to each other and understand clearly what the other wishes to tell us simply by opening our minds to them. The communicative effort is strengthened and supported by the feelings of love we have for each other, and by the common desire we have to work for the Divine Plan and to bring that ideal into the physical level. We do have actual meetings and discussions where we meet face-to-face, but much of what we say has already been said before that. It is merely a confirmation of what has gone before in other levels of communication besides the physical one. I am speaking relatively here when I say physical, because we work at the physical level through the fifth dimension and that is really the farthest into the physical that we go.

We work a great deal on the sixth and seventh dimensions. These are the levels where we can attune to the Divine Ideal which is coming from the Galactic Center. This is where we pick up the plans which they have for the Earth and where we receive our guidance from them. This is really telepathy that we are talking about here. It's something which is being developed on the Earth and all of you use probably more than you are aware. This is a broad view of telepathy which includes a communication of feelings as well as thoughts. It involves the use of the heart and a connection that is formed through love.

You may have at times experienced a communication over a distance from a loved one when there was trouble. This could be an awareness of an experience they were going through, or it could be a message that they need you, or an awareness that something needs to be done on your part. The bond of love makes the connection much stronger and allows you to reach out to them, so you can receive their thoughts when they send them to you. When the spiritual teachers connect with you on occasion to bring you a message, their love is the medium which carries the thought to you. Your love for them is what allows you to receive the message.

So, love is a very important part of communication. There are those who can influence the minds of others without love and who do so for their own purposes. This is a negative use of personal power and is not what I am discussing. It is not in alignment with the ideal and it will cause spiritual difficulty for these individuals eventually. They will have to learn that it is not appropriate and that communication, just as any other sharing process, must be beneficial to both parties before it is ethically valid. Communication is done ideally with the heart as well as with the mind. Both of these must be used in order to make a good connection and in order to share the knowledge or the message between you.

My message to you is to use love and your heart in all of your communications with others. This allows a sharing between you which creates an intensification and multiplication of the light as it flows through you into the Earth. Using your heart in the communication is another way of helping the Earth. Any time you are using love as a physical being, you are bringing love into the Earth. Your ability to do this determines the clarity of the message and determines the quality or the magnitude of the light that you are able to give to the Earth through the process.

Your heart, if used consciously, can help you to communicate more clearly. It shows you, through your response and theirs, the quality of the message you are sending. As others respond to what you send them, and as you respond to what they send back, your heart receives a message which it can use to decide what you need to do to communicate more clearly.

The mind helps in this process, also. It helps to analyze the results and helps you to clarify or correct the message which you are sending. But the mind alone cannot make the connection that is needed here. The use of the heart in communication expands the communication beyond mere words or mere expression of your desire into a light exchange which operates on many levels. This allows you to share your strengths as creators with each other and allows you to utilize that sharing for growth and expansion of your light abilities on the Earth.

Another quality of clear communication is visual contact. An eye-to-eye contact allows the other to know they have your full attention. It also allows you to see into their heart more clearly and it activates that heart flow. If there is fear within you of using your heart in communication with others, this may be difficult for you to do. If this is true, I would suggest that you make an effort to learn to trust the communicative process and learn to utilize a flow from your heart through visual eye-to-eye contact. Allow your heart to expand as you look into the other person's eyes, and allow your trust to make the process easier for you.

There have been many times on the Earth when it was a grave offense to look another person in the eye. It was a sign that you wished to dominate them or that you wished to harm them in some way. It still can be a symbol of aggression for those who have violent tendencies within themselves. If one can learn to transmute this aggressiveness into love, the process becomes a positive and supportive one. There are very few places remaining on the Earth where you can be put to death for looking someone in the eye. Although this has happened to some of you in the past, you can trust and know that it will not happen again.

The eyes are called the windows of the soul. It is time for humanity to use them in that way. It's time for you to be able to share with others the love of your soul that is pouring into your hearts, and which is destined to be a part of your life. You can do this by allowing the love in your heart to shine from your eyes and visualize the natural connection there. Feel the love flowing from your heart through your eyes to everything that you look at. I think that this exercise alone, if you work at it, could cause enormous transformation within your relationships with others. You can practice feeling the soul's presence within yourself, radiating from your heart and shining through your eyes. This allows communicative experiences with others to be loving and satisfying for all involved.

As you learn to feel the presence of those of us who dwell on the inner planes, and who wish to work through you within physical existence, looking others in the eye allows us to share more clearly our love with those with whom you communicate. It allows us to see more clearly into their soul from a physical level. It can be very helpful to us in aiding them, just as we aid you when you allow us to be a part of your lives. A kind look and a smile can perhaps do more than a thousand words in moving another toward the goal of recognizing their divine potential. A loving glance can do more than many words to let another understand that they are loved, that they are accepted and that their friendship is of value to you.

Perhaps it is difficult for you to realize the importance of utilizing love in your communications when you are at the physical level. If you practice this as I suggest and learn to use your heart in communication, then I think you will begin to see what I mean. You will learn far more than what I have stated here about the benefits and the power of love in communications.

It is time for the Earth to begin to recognize the existence and the usefulness of other levels besides the physical. This is one way to help the Earth to move into the ability to do that. Each one of you is a part of the Earth. As you learn to utilize love in every facet of your life, the Earth itself becomes more loving. It moves more easily with the flow of divine love which is surrounding and interpenetrating all of the Earth's energies and guiding its movements.

I thank you very much for this opportunity to speak with you. I am sending you much love with the hope that it will support you in your use of love in communication.

Thank you.

Meditation

Imagine that I am standing in front of you. I have on a purple robe and a purple turban on my head with an amethyst in it. I am holding a goblet made of amethyst and offering it to you. You can drink as much as you want of the contents of this goblet. It will never be empty. You may even be able to see it filling itself. You can pour it over you if you like. Then just sit quietly and allow the new energy you have taken in to heal and balance you. Allow it to go to any part of your body that needs it. It contains the substance of new shapes and ideas which are forming in your cells. When they are complete, they will begin to be available to you. Every time you take a drink of water, imagine that this energy is being reenergized in you.

St. Germaine

Using the Violet Ray

Greetings, my friends. Many of you know me as one who has been working with your Earth for a long time, sometimes in a very visible way. I am working in many ways now, some of them visible, some of them invisible.

My primary task, as a member of your Earth Hierarchy, is to bring you the light of the Violet Ray and to focus it for Earth so you can utilize it as a part of your growth and evolution. Since the Violet Ray is such an important part of what I am doing, I am going to talk about that.

The Violet Ray is the one that is bringing the light of transformation. It is the color that most allows you to move forward. It helps you let go of what is no longer needed and take advantage of the opportunities that are coming to you. It helps use more of your potentialities and more of your strengths as creative beings. The Violet Ray is really stimulating the growth of creativity on the Earth. It is doing this, not only through its own innate properties, but because it is an introduction to the higher rays, the higher vibrational energies that are available to the Earth.

These energies have always come to you through the sunlight but now they are beginning to come from other sources in your galaxy, primarily from the Galactic Center. The Galactic Center is something that has not been recognized much on the Earth until now, because humanity and the Earth have really been working on centering themselves as a part of the solar system. You have been working to develop your hearts, so you can use the light of your soul creatively in your life. Now that your creativity is more secure and you are beginning to take more responsibility for your own lives and your planet, this new doorway has opened which allows you to see beyond your purposes as a planet or as a solar system. These purposes that we are showing you now are helping you expand your vision of yourselves as cosmic beings who create your Earth, who create your solar system, and who even create what is beyond that. That you can create a galaxy may be a difficult concept for you to grasp. This is a new step for you.

It is time for you to open yourself to the creative possibilities that you have on the Earth. It is time for you to expand past the mere personal concerns that have limited you for so long. It is time for you to begin to see yourself as a part of a group, called humanity, as a part of a solar system, and truly, as an integral part of a galaxy. What happens on the Earth is very important to the whole galaxy and to the whole universe. You may be compared in size to one cell within the universe. Yet, the impact that one cell can make is extremely important, especially when it is expanding as rapidly in light as the Earth is now.

The radiance of this particular planet is affecting the solar system and the galaxy. Its radiance is being noted and it is becoming a focus of attention for the whole universe, more specifically, for this galactic sector. It is time now for the Earth to become a functioning part of the galaxy, a part of this cosmic being who knows who it is, and what its purpose is. That is the focus of the Violet Ray, to bring you this broader perspective of what you are, who you are, and of your place in the universe.

Surrounding yourself with the violet light in meditation will help you expand your awareness. You can utilize amethyst crystals, purple fluorite crystals, and other purple stones to aid you in attuning your-self to the new vibrational levels that are available within the light, particularly within this Violet Ray. Each purple crystal helps you to attune to it in a different way. Each level you reach in meditation will help you utilize this light of the Violet Ray in your life. The Violet Ray can help you understand your part in the Plan and to find your place within this evolving perspective of Earth's creativity.

I'm not saying that other colors are not important. Blue and pink are still very important for helping you understand yourselves as lov-ing, heart-centered beings. Green is very important for you to use in connecting to the Earth and in understanding how much your creativ-ity is rooted within the Earth itself. But the Violet Ray will help you to evolve beyond the foundation of this understanding and help you move into an acceptance of yourselves as cosmic cocreators who have come to the Earth to aid Source in expanding Its creativity in this particular way.

I am not presently within physical existence in a consistent man-ner. However, I do come from time to time for specific purposes or to anchor specific parts of my energy flow, my Violet Ray into the Earth. This is a time- and energy-consuming procedure, so I am grateful to all of you who help me anchor the Violet Ray into the Earth. This enables me to use your physical structures instead of my own for this purpose. Each time one of you uses the Violet Ray in your meditation to clear your physical structure, each time you bring the Violet Ray through yourselves and focus it into the Earth to aid in healing and clearing the

Earth, you help me to use my resources more efficiently for the planet.

One of my purposes in bringing this message to you is to ask you to use the Violet Ray as much as you can in your meditation. See not only violet, but much iridescence, white and silver, and many sparkles of gold. The Violet Ray is becoming more alive, and it is being used more often as a balanced light format to bring a higher expression of light energy to the Earth. Use the sparkles of silver, to make it flow more easily into the dark corners and into the blocked areas of your body that need to be cleansed and opened. See the violet light flowing into every cell of your physical body to stimulate the transformation into light. Use it often in your hearts, for through the flow of you heart energies this Violet Ray can be directed to the point where it is most needed.

Your heart is the part of you that is connected to the whole of humanity and to the heart of the Earth itself. Therefore, the more you use your heart in service to the Earth, the more effective it will become in attuning to what the Earth and humanity need. Then it can direct those higher energies to the particular place where they are needed.

You could say I am organizing humanity, as much as possible, into one integrated system for bringing this Violet Ray to the Earth. By anchoring into the Earth through humanity, we can bring the Plan to the physical level of Earth.

The Violet Ray is, perhaps more than any ray, the architect of the New Age. It is the ray of transformation. It is the energy which is clearing out what is no longer needed, to prepare the foundation of the New Age. As you use the Violet Ray, you are bringing out the Plan that is encoded within each particle of light. As this ray and its particles of light which contain the Plan are focused within physical existence, the Plan becomes more and more a part of physical existence, the Earth, and each of you. This Plan carries the blueprint for a perfect physical structure, a healthier, more efficient body and a more satisfying life for each of you. It contains the blueprint for an Earth which supports all of its kingdoms in great abundance and provides a means of realizing their creative efforts completely, so they can evolve and grow as Creators. Each individual on the Earth will be able to develop his own particular creative strength. Each will be able to make his own creative contribution and fulfill his purposes as a part of physical existence.

Encoded within this Violet Ray are the blueprints for a new social order, for new political orders, for a new monetary system, all of which will be more supportive and beneficial to the whole of humanity. It contains the blueprint for new cities and new ways of utilizing the Earth's resources which will be in harmony with the Earth's purposes and its growth and evolution. It carries the blueprint for growth within humanity which will allow each to live in harmony with the others and with the Earth, without the misperception of giving up what they need when they share with another. Many of you are now praying and asking for help for the Earth. You are asking for peace. You are praying for more love to be available on the planet. Your prayers are being answered through the light and through the Plan which is coming to you as part of this Violet Ray. Through recognizing this Violet Ray and using it in your life as light, you will be receiving your answer to your prayers. You will be planting new seeds of opportunity on your Earth through creative expression. This is known as the New Age.

Anytime you pray or ask for help from any of the teachers, the Angelic Kingdom, or from what you perceive as God, you will always receive an answer. Sometimes you may not recognize the form this answer takes. By utilizing the Violet Ray as something you know is coming to the Earth to serve you and help you move forward, you will be allowing your prayers to be answered at the physical level. You will be allowing yourself to utilize a vehicle that is here to help you and serve you. This vehicle is available to you any time, if you allow it to come through you. So, you might say, that connecting into the Violet Ray is a means of connecting into the answers to your prayers for a more peaceful and harmonious life on Earth and for a more loving sharing of its resources with all of its kingdoms.

I know many of you personally. I know you recognize me as a friend and as a teacher. I would be honored if you would attune to me and to the Violet Ray, in order to help your Earth and yourselves move forward into the New Age. I thank all of you for your service as light bearers on the Earth. I am grateful to be able to speak with you and for having the opportunity to make this connection with you. I will be happy to help you use this Violet Ray and develop your own spiritual potentials and your understanding of yourselves as divine creative beings.

My love to you. I am grateful for your prayers and your acceptance of my light on the Earth. Thank you.

Exercise

Pretend you are going to the post office to get a letter. Take it home with you and open it. As you do so, light comes from it that surrounds you and goes into your head. You have just gotten a light message. Don't try too hard to read it. Just allow it to be there. It will stimulate your own thoughts and rearrange them into different ideas. Some of what is going through your mind will be new. Just let everything come. If questions come up, ask them and allow the answers to be part of the flow. You might want to write down things that seem important or you can record all your thoughts into a tape recorder.

If you do this regularly, the results will vary. Sometimes you will get specific messages. Other times you may need to sort out personal things and the ideas will be centered around you and will help you do this.

Rowena

Personal Spiritual Guidance

Greetings, my beloved friends. I am Rowena. I am the captain of a ship and the leader of a rather large fleet that works from higher dimensions around the Earth and for the Earth. Many of you are my friends, and many of you have been on my ship. My purpose is to serve as a "personnel director" for the lightworkers who are working with Ashtar on nonphysical levels and on Earth.

My job is to keep track of everyone working with us by maintaining a record of their genetic codes and light structure in a computerized data bank which we maintain. In this way, we know where you are and what you are doing at each moment. More importantly, we know what progress you are making. When you make an important step in your growth or when you make some important realization about who you are and how you are here to serve the Earth, we are aware of it. We then make adjustments in the light format we are sending you to help you move to the next step. Many times, you are brought to my ship during sleep or in a higher state for what you might call rebriefing and reassignment. Some of you consciously remember being on my ship, being interviewed, being counseled and being given specific assignments.

When necessary, I also refer you to specific other groups within the Space Command for physical healing, for emotional balancing or for assignment to various classes which will aid you in your work on the Earth. You may not remember all of what you are learning, but in your conscious physical life on Earth you might become conscious of a new urge to study some new subject, for example. As you pursue this study, you will find that many things come to you rather easily, and that you have some knowledge beyond what you are learning in your studies on the Earth. This is because you are paralleling in your Earth studies what you are doing on the higher levels of your awareness. I receive reports when you complete your classes or your healing sessions. Then I notify your teachers who need to be appraised of your progress. I coordinate what they know with what I have recorded.

I would like to be able to communicate with some of you on an individual basis. Then I can help you understand more clearly all of what is available to you and help you understand more of the strengths that you have within yourself. I can see on my computer the gains you have made in past lives. I have a good record of your particular strengths. Many times the jobs that you have been given are chosen so that you can recognize and develop the strengths that are latent and forgotten within you. So, if you seem to be struggling with some new opportunity which has come to you and from which you feel you have something to gain, but for which you are not yet qualified, allow yourself to reach within and stretch into finding some of those strengths which you already have. Through my energies I can help you connect into some of those strengths that you have forgotten, and help you find and use them more easily within your life now.

I also want very much for all of you to know how much love and support there is available to you on the levels of awareness which are not so easily available to you within physical existence. As you learn to turn inward and expand into more of what you are, more of this becomes available to you. I would like to help you look inward by helping you understand and see more clearly where it is that you are going as you venture inward into yourself and outward into more of your potential.

We are here to spiritually support your creative efforts and to help you bring the spiritual plan to the Earth so you may find your place within it. For many of you, just knowing that this support is available will be a great help to you. For others, it will answer many questions, perhaps explain strange dreams, perceptions and memories within you which you have not been able to interpret. It will also help you understand more clearly the vast amount of help you get when you allow yourself to be supported by the Earth. We are as much a part of the Earth as you, even though we are not within physical existence. We are among those many spiritual levels of the Earth, of which you are only now beginning to be aware, but which are as much a part of your Earth as you are.

There are many beings within my fleet who would like to be able to communicate with you. Many of them are your friends and co-workers with whom you have worked for many lifetimes. If you are communicating in as many ways as you can, with both those on the Earth and those within the highest planes, we can expand this creative network which we use to support each other's creativity. We can all move forward as a united group to bring a clearer understanding of the wonderful spiritual potential that is available within the Earth and the marvelous opportunity that we have to create a more beautiful and satisfying Earth experience for all, according to our Source Plan.

My deepest love to you, my dear ones. You are all within my

heart. I send you my love and I ask only that you share that love with all with whom you come in contact. Thank you.

Exercise/Meditation

Imagine your soul as a woman who embodies all the best that any woman can be. She is standing in front of you and has some ideas about how she can help you become more whole. She knows you very well and can help you with any problem. Listen for her ideas. Let her place them in you wherever they will help the most. You may not realize exactly what she is doing or saying until some later time.

Now imagine your soul as a man who is all the best any man can be. He too is here and has ideas and suggestions for your growth and healing. Allow him to give you what he offers, as you did the woman.

Now see the two coming together and blending their energies. They surround you with their light. They symbolize your potential for balanced wholeness. They can help you integrate any parts of yourself which have become separated from the flow of the life you wish to create for yourself. Talk to them often. No one else is as important to them as you.

Athena

Sexual Equality

Greetings, my friends. I am Athena. I work with Ashtar as a leader in what you call the Space Command. I consider myself a lightworker just like you. I am working from a slightly different dimensional perspective, but I am a part of the Earth and am concerned with her evolution just as you are. I am also very concerned with aiding humanity as a part of the Earth in its evolution now.

I have spent many, many eons on your Earth and feel as though I am very much a part of it, as a feminine or receptive representation of the Source flow, the mother qualities, the nurturing and creative potentials that are a part of your Earth and what she represents.

Your Earth is regarded as a feminine planet, because she so outstandingly represents the creative potential that is available within physical existence. She is very open to the guidance and direction and inspiration of the Father or Source. She is very open to using the Source Energy to serve as a means of expressing the creative Will of Source. She considers herself to be a part of the creative field which Source has formed for exploring the potentials within Itself. Each one of you is part of this creative field also. As creations of Source, you have been put here to explore its creative possibilities. You are directed by Its Divine Will as It comes through you in the shape of the Plan for the Earth.

Each of you, whether you are in a male or female body, are here to learn to serve as creative representatives of Source within this particular field of experience. I was among the very first humans to come to the Earth. I have been with her ever since, although I have experienced some periods on other planets during that time as well.

I have watched your Earth grow and I have watched humanity evolve with her. I have been a queen many times just as you have, and I have also been a slave, a servant and a beggar. Most of my lifetimes were spent as an ordinary person, working to do my part within the society to which I belonged to further the work of Spirit as much as I could allow It to come through me.

During the period of Atlantis on your Earth, I worked closely with Ashtar. This was my final physical lifetime. During that lifetime, we both were able to bring together all of our physical experiences and integrate them into our divine perspective, so that we no longer needed to work within the dense, physical aspects of life in order to be a part of all that was going on. We had been together before and our energies complemented each other very well. We continue to do so. I am sometimes regarded as the female polarity of the Ashtar energy, but that is not quite accurate, as I am a unique individual in my own right, not simply a subsidiary of that energy which is Ashtar. Our perspectives are so similar that we see as one being, but that is not unique at the spiritual levels. Everyone who reaches that level is able to tune into the whole and relate to it in a way that allows him or her to make it their own.

I am particularly interested in helping the Earth, and all of those within her, to achieve a more balanced polarity perspective. In short, I am working now to achieve equality between the sexes. I have been working through certain groups which attune to my energies. We are working with very young children in kindergarten, or even younger, to plant the seeds of sexual equality at an early age when it is so important. I am not the only one doing this but it is a very important part of my work. I think we are making progress. I think the young people today show a great deal less prejudice against women and a great deal more recognition that feminine qualities are important in creating a balanced outlook, personality, and way of working with the Earth and her energies.

Your Earth is learning, just as you are, that being feminine or being receptive does not mean that you must always be dominated by the will of another. What it does mean is that you allow that creative potential within you to be stimulated by the Divine Plan. This creates a movement and a growth within you that expands and evolves into a specific purpose, that progresses a particular idea or that carries out a specific plan on the Earth.

Men and women on the Earth are both learning to be receptive to this divine will and to respond to it in a way that is creative and in alignment with the Plan. On your Earth and in this universe, we have chosen to experience these dynamic and receptive qualities as separate, but sexual differences are present only at the physical and etheric levels. At the spiritual levels, we are all both dynamic and receptive. You are growing into a greater awareness of your divine potential on the Earth now. As you do this, you need to become aware that both of these polarities are present within you and that they need to be balanced. Each polarity needs to be utilized equally in your creative efforts. If you are a woman, you will never be creative if you simply allow yourself to receive the male energy. You must also respond to it in a way which creates new movement. A male cannot be creative if he only stimulates and does not respond and allow the growth that is the natural result of this stimulation.

An idea can grow into an actual structure on this Earth through a man or a woman, just as a child is conceived and born within a woman's body. The woman's body can be symbolic for the spiritual potentialities that are available within all of humanity, male and female. It is symbolic of nurturing the creative seeds that are available within each one of you, that each one of you has brought to the Earth to use in this particular creative experience. Each one of you carries the seeds of the New Age which are ready to be stimulated and brought to life by the light of the Plan, and supported by the combined male and female energies of all of humanity. Each of you has a specific seed to contribute to the New Age. When all of these seeds begin to grow, the New Age will come into being on your planet.

Your Earth has understood since its beginning that her role was to serve as a garden in which Source could plant many seeds and bring them to life. Earth knows that it is symbolizing an Eden for the entire universe, a place where creativity has a special opportunity to expand in new ways. She is learning that she has a right to control and to choose what takes place within her, which seeds are stimulated, how they should be supported and nurtured, and in what directions they should be allowed to grow. She is realizing that she no longer needs to serve as prey for other creative systems to support their desires.

Earth can choose the means of bringing to life those creative seeds within her. She has chosen now to call forth a great variety of spiritual entities, and to ask them to bring their perspective of the Plan so she can choose one of them to work with and to utilize within herself. What this means practically is that the Earth is no longer open to pirates and profiteers who seek only to exploit her. She is closing the doors to them, and opening to the creative potential of those who come with higher, more spiritual purposes and who wish to serve Earth rather than exploit her.

The doors have not completely closed. The Earth is waiting for humanity to aid her and to see that, as part of the Earth, it can choose with whom it works and how the work is done. As humanity learns to balance the male and female aspects within themselves as individuals, Earth is learning to balance the dynamic and receptive qualities within herself as a dynamic creative being.

That is how the New Age will be built. It will be built on a foundation of sexual equality that allows each individual to receive the ideal that the Plan represents and to use all of his or her personal resources to bring it about. This work will be done within the cooperative effort of a group focus. The receptive qualities in each will allow the dynamic qualities of the group to stimulate the creative productivity of the group more than was ever possible before.

In order to further understand the balancing of the sexes on the Earth, I would ask each of you to meditate from time to time on that balance within yourself. Know that each of you can be loving, nurturing and joyous in your support of the whole, and at the same time be dynamic stimulators of your own creativity and the creativity of others.

You can be gentle and yet forceful and confident in your own strengths. You can be nurturing and yet allow others to support you in areas where they are strong and you are weak, while you support their weak areas with your strong ones. You can be loving and compassionate without compromising the strengths of the creative potential within you. You can share your strengths with others without diminishing them, because they also share their strengths which you recognize.

You can look at your weaknesses without diminishing yourself, because behind every weakness, there is a potential for great strength which can be brought forth through the help of others who are willing to work with you and support you, just as you support them. There is a balancing that moves much faster as you work together as a group and share your strengths and help each other in a nonjudging, understanding way, accepting that each of us has areas that need work, just as each of us has strengths to share in the whole.

See yourselves as beings who are both female and male, capable of existing within a body that is either male or female, yet carrying the spiritual potential of completeness from a higher level. When enough of you have seen this clearly within yourselves, those areas of the Earth which are somewhat backward in their understanding will have no choice but to move forward and let go of their misbeliefs which do not allow both sexes to be equally creative on the Earth.

If you would like to attune to me and my energies, I would be happy to share my knowledge and my goals with you. I work with a very large group of spiritual beings within your Space Command on the less physical levels of your Earth planes. We are all interested in bringing about a balance of the polarities on the Earth that allows sexual equality. Our goal is that each individual on the Earth will have an opportunity to be equally creative within this New Age.

I have great love for each one of you, great respect for the work you are doing on the Earth and much gratitude for the dedication with which you are seeking to bring forth light to her. I am pleased to be a part of this Earth experience and grateful for the opportunities she has given me to serve.

Thank you for this opportunity to speak with you. I hope to continue working with humanity and the Earth at a deeper level as we align more and more closely with the Plan Source has for her. I am your friend and co-worker who has great love for each of you.

Exercise

Imagine that you can connect with my ship by means of a special radio-telephone. Next to you imagine a receiver with a set of headphones. Put on the headset and turn on the receiver. Tune it to my light frequency or set the dial on "Cosima." You will be able to pick up my thoughts or those of one of my friends in your mind and we will be able to pick up yours. If you have some sort of crystal headband, that would make a very good receiver. Eventually you will no longer need these devices, but they may help you develop your channeling connection.

Cosima

A New Understanding of Time and Space

Greetings, I am Cosima. I am a "Space Being," which means I exist in a dimension different from yours, but still very much a part of Earth. I am living and working on a large spaceship which has come from beyond your universe. It is shaped something like a toy top and is run by a computer system at the Galactic Center, so there is very little actual piloting that needs to be done. There are emergency controls to be used, if necessary, but the possibility that these will be needed is very slight.

I lead the people within the ship rather than actually being the commander of the ship itself. My people come from diverse places within creation and have been called by your Galactic Center to come and help at a crucial point in Earth's evolution. We all volunteered and are quite excited about being here at such an important time. We work in cooperation with the Galactic Center. As we come here, we "check-in" with the Galactic Center and the Ashtar Commands. All of our activities are coordinated through their computer systems, so each ship in all of the commands always knows what the other is doing and each ship knows its place within the whole Plan. Our job involves determining the energy format and the frequency needs of the Earth at a particular time. We use that knowledge, that blueprint, for the Earth and energize it as our contribution to the Plan for the whole Earth.

Your universe is operating at a slightly lower density or frequency than ours and time is slower here. One thing we are seeking to bring is an expanded viewpoint of time and of "What Is" as well as what you can be within The Whole. Our particular focus is bringing through an adjustment in time awareness on the Earth which allows it to move more easily into the fourth dimension and to flow with that fourth-dimensional understanding. This allows the transition into an expanded awareness of yourselves as divine beings in the sense that you can control the passage of time within your own perceptions and on your own planet. The effects of this may not be immediately apparent to you, although I think you can all relate to the fact that time seems to be moving much more rapidly than it has been. This is because of an acceleration effect in the energy format which the Earth is utilizing now. We are seeking to help you and the Earth adjust to this new frequency, through a clearer understanding of time and what it really is.

Time, of course, is a means of stepping down light activities or light occurrences so that you can look at them as isolated events. In reality, every event within your life occurs at precisely the same moment in the Eternal Now, but you look at it as an evolvement or development of the one that came before. This is a way of learning what you are and how you evolve out of the essence of what you are.

Therefore, time allows you to spread out a very large picture and divide it up into small increments which have a specific meaning for you and which are more easily understood. Eventually, you will bring this picture back into its wholeness, putting the pieces together so you can look, in a new way, at the meaning of each in relationship to the Whole.

This expanded viewpoint of time which we are bringing forth is one means of doing that. It helps you integrate your Earth experiences, your knowledge and your understanding into the greater whole of what you are as a creative being. Therefore, it helps you bring together your strengths and abilities into your own understanding of your own creativity.

Your scientists and physicists are unfolding the meaning and relationship between space and time. This reflects a spiritual understanding that is present within all of you of how you relate to time and space. Your scientific developments now are reflecting your own development as spiritual beings as you begin to see more potentials within yourselves and to utilize more of the potentials that you have. We are, of course, working on only one aspect of this potential and that is understanding time and how to bring an understanding of it into a meaningful whole.

I would like to communicate with many individuals on Earth in this matter of understanding yourselves as beings within an expanded viewpoint of time. By working through many channels, I can bring through a broader picture of what it is we are trying to do for the Earth and how we are trying to work with her. Each of you will bring through a slightly different way of looking at this and will contribute in your special way to the understanding of the whole.

You can work with that knowledge and use it in a way that allows you to expand your own understanding of the Earth, time and yourselves. You can visualize me within the ship or you can use my picture. That can be very helpful for some of you. All that is actually necessary is for you to think of my name and allow the light energy that is myself to come through your channel. Then begin to open to an understanding of time as we are bringing it from the Galactic Center.

I, and those on my ship, bring our special talents as our contribution from our universe to your Galactic Center and the Earth. We bring them with much joy and love and seek to work as friends and partners with you.

Meditation

Let's assume for now that Source is a single point from which radiates a multitude of light streams. One of these light streams is you. Right now your consciousness may be focused in the part of the light stream which seems far from Source. But, since the whole stream is you, you can move to any place in it you wish. Try moving along the stream back toward Source. Go as far as you choose and absorb the energy of that point into your whole being. Go all the way into Source and know that you have a right to be there and take the love that is there into yourself.

If you go far enough out on this stream, you will always come back to Source. See how that feels. This stream of light is love, your love, the Creator's love. You can use it, flow with it, dance with it, play in it, whatever you choose. You can even change its direction and intersect other streams. Try it. It can be fun. Wherever you go, you will find other light streams made of love. When you come back to your starting point you may have realized that you are more than you see or feel in this point in space and time.

Master Kuthumi

Learning to Be Love

W hat joy it brings me to be able to speak to you here. I know this is going to allow me to communicate with some of you more clearly than I have before.

My job as a part of your Planetary Hierarchy is to support and help the Christ in any way that I can. He is the World Teacher and I am helping Him to bring a greater understanding of love and wisdom to the Earth now. The Earth is created from love and is composed of love. It is love that she needs now to heal her and allow her to become the new being that she wants to be. All of you, as a part of the Earth, are love also.

As conscious beings, it is your opportunity to evolve the wisdom that allows you to use this love creatively. Love and wisdom cannot be separated. They are what Source is, they are what creation is, they are what you are in every cell of your being. Love is the creative material with which you work. Wisdom organizes it into the forms with which you create.

You haven't always understood that you are love, but as you grow and evolve in your understanding of what you are, you discover more and more that that is the most important element with which you can work now. We of your Planetary Hierarchy have always been here, working to help you to make that realization, and to help you learn to use love and wisdom in your lives as a part of Source's Plan for the Earth.

I became an active member of your Planetary Hierarchy about 5000 years ago. But I have returned to physical existence a number of times since then to help bring a greater awareness of love and wisdom to the Earth. As the builder of the Taj Mahal, I tried to show how love can be expressed as beauty and as a physical part of your Earth. As Pythagoras, I tried to show that love can exist as a scientific or mathematical framework for existence on Earth. As one of the three wise men, I sought to prepare the way for the coming of more love as light to the Earth. During the Middle Ages, I came very briefly as a priest in France who wrote a short book on love.

I have known many of you in physical existence and worked with you as a teacher and as a fellow traveler along the path. Many of you may recognize me now as someone who has been with you often as a guide from the spiritual kingdom who supports you at times of great need or great decision. It is my job to support you with my love and wisdom whenever you need it and can accept it. I do this with great joy and gratitude that I am able to serve in this way. I have learned a great deal from each one of you and I have grown with you.

There is a great need now for individuals on the Earth who can live as expressions of the Creator's love, and who can share that love within a group so that the group becomes the creative love focus for the Plan. It is no longer enough to simply love yourself and love others. Although that is certainly an important first step, what is more important now is to be able to share your love and your strengths with the group. Look at yourself as part of the group that is bringing forth a part of the Plan on the Earth. This is the only way now that you will be able to utilize your strengths to the fullest and to accomplish your purposes on the Earth. You need the support of others because no one person has the key to the New Age.

You can say that love is the key to achieving your potential, and accepting Christ in your hearts is the key to achieving your purpose. But, love is expressed through many hearts and minds, as many strengths and many talents. It is the integration of the diversity of strengths and talents which forms the whole potential of love wisdom for this planet and which allows it to reach completion.

I want to help each of you learn to recognize and use your strengths, so you can do your part in putting the Plan for the New Age on Earth into action. There are many groups on the Earth now that are working toward this goal. I am aware of each one of them, and I help them in any way that I can. As much as they are open to spiritual guidance, we can bring the inspiration that is needed to move the work of each group forward. As you open your meetings with prayer or meditation, my energies and the energies of the Christ are there to support and inspire you. We are a link into the greater expression of the Plan for the Earth as conceived and brought to us by our Heavenly Father, the Planetary Logos.

There is still a great deal of work to be done on your Earth before it is ready to finally enter the New Age. There are still some things on the Earth which are not understood and which are seen as darkness. Each one of you, as part of the Earth, has chosen to look at some bit or part of this darkness. During your many lifetimes on your Earth, you have incorporated a part of this darkness into your cellular level, and, in a sense, made it your own so that you may clear it, turn it into light and release the creative potential that is there. That is what you are all doing now as you clear yourselves. You are also clearing the Earth of its inability to understand completely the light potential that is here. That is why you have so much help now as a part of the Earth group. As each of you clears the darkness within you and understands more of the light that is there, you create a forward movement for light on the Earth which helps others to clear their little bit of darkness from within themselves also.

There is no one on the Earth within physical existence or the spiritual kingdom, such as those of us within the Hierarchy, who are not dealing with this darkness or have not dealt with it in the past. It is a part of becoming physical; it is a part of what the Creator asks you to do when He gives you the opportunity to enter physical existence. You build great strengths in your understanding of light by looking at what is not yet seen as light and incorporating it as light into the framework of what you are. So, this process begins by integrating something that is not understood into your light framework, then transforming it, as a part of what you are, into a flow that is completely light and absolutely understood as a part of Source. There is really no evil on the Earth, there is simply that part of Source that has not been understood, has not been integrated as light and therefore is not available to you to use creatively.

As long as you have an individual consciousness, there is some part of Source that is not understood. The Earth now is reaching a new level of understanding itself as light and as a part of Source. This level of understanding will provide the foundation for an even greater awareness of love as light through the use of wisdom in the future. The Earth is here to share this with you and provide the material that you need to work with in evolving your understanding of yourself as cocreators.

My message to you now is that there can never be too much love on the Earth. Source, in Its wisdom, has provided an infinite supply of it. As you learn to use more and more love, you approach the infinity of Source within yourself. You don't have to be a Master of Wisdom to use this love now. You don't have to be able to use it according to your own ideas of perfection, you simply have to use it as much as you can in your life.

Act as though you are using love, even if you don't feel like it on that day. Think about a difficult situation, and think about what it would be like to act as love in that situation and then try to act that way in a similar situation. The more you act as if you are love, the more you use it, the more you find there is love within you, the more it will flow forth and begin to wash away the doubt about your ability to use it. You are love, even though you don't always feel like it. The only way to completely understand yourself as love is to keep using it and keep learning about what it will accomplish when you use it.

The same is true for learning to use joy and peacefulness and trust in your lives. You aren't expected to understand them fully from the beginning. What we suggest is that you simply use them whenever possible. That will allow you to understand them, and you will find them growing within you so that, more and more, you discover that you are loved, you are joyful, you are peaceful, you do trust.

You are wholly composed of Source and what It is. What is not love, joy, peace, contentment, compassion within you is simply what you have not yet understood. Love what you do not understand within yourself and it will become light. I, and the rest of your spiritual teachers, will be here to greet you when the realization of that light finally dawns within you and allows you to step into the wholeness of what you are. I see that as if it already were true, and I welcome you now into the Kingdom of Light which love and wisdom make possible on your Earth now.

Meditation

You are totally surrounded by love. It caresses you, supports you and fills you. It is all there is and you are the center of it. Try to feel this and know it. Trust yourself to it completely. You and love are a unit of consciousness, like a ball of energy, perhaps. Let this ball expand slowly, taking in everything around you. Look at specific things as they become part of this consciousness that is you. See love dissolve any negativity. Only love is left to become part of the expanding you.

The Elohim

Becoming the Cocreator within You

W e are the Elohim. We are the highest essence of your true selves. We exist as a unit which is fully aware of our oneness with Source, as cocreators for all that is. We are the total essence of all that is creative within your universe. We greet you now with great love, with great joy and with great enthusiasm, for the beautiful light that is growing within each of you. You could say we are God-essence, because, in a very real way, we are that most intimate, most central portion of yourself, the central spark of life which is your inherent divinity. We are basically all that you are. Full awareness of Elohim is what you are seeking to become. The ability to use all of our knowledge and powers is one of the things you are learning on the Earth. Our energies comprise all of physical existence and that includes the densest physical part of it. It includes the Earth under your feet, the substance of which you are composed, and every aspect of your physical lives as well as your inner, more spiritual lives.

What you are doing on the Earth is seeking to blend the spiritual awareness that is within each part of you into a wholeness that allows you to see yourselves as divine light, as totally spiritual beings, and as creators of your own world. We are always fully present on your world. We never leave, we have never gone. You have not always recognized us, and your Earth has not always allowed itself to fully utilize our light. Now a fuller realization that we are here is coming to your Earth. We are available and we are truly a part of what you are. Your Earth provides the opportunity for you to expand your knowledge of all that you are. There is a true partnership here between you and your Earth, which allows you each to develop most fully your cocreative abilities. This partnership allows you to see more clearly how to create as divine beings and how to allow the creative spirit to come through you clearly.

Source has given us many worlds in which to experience this growth of creativity. It has given us many ways of learning to express our creativity. It has given us an infinity of time in which to do this. The Source has said, "I give you all that I am, and all I ask in return is that you use it to create something new and something more wonderful than has existed before." On Earth, this means each day can be a new expression of the beauty that is within you and of the ability to create something which is always showing more clearly the Source quality that is within it. It means each thing you do becomes more of an expression of all that you are. It means you can continually grow in your ability to express the beauty and truth of Source, through your life and through your understanding and awareness.

When we say you are cocreators with your Earth, we mean this: the Earth itself is a heavenly, divine being, one that is evolving and growing in its understanding of all that it is just as you are. It is composed of atoms, each of which is an aspect of Source. Each has a different way of expressing what Source is, and each had its own purpose in growing and evolving as divine light. As you become associated with the Earth and as you become a part of it, you learn to use Earth's resources which have been formed into soil, rocks and minerals, plants, animals, your fellow humans, even those on the spiritual level, who are your teachers, and your guides. They are all there to help you whenever you need it and they all want to work with you.

As cocreators you learn to work with all of this Source material which is available to you. You learn to use it in a wise and balanced way. You learn to use it by understanding completely that it is divine just as you are, and that it is available to cooperate with you in a creative effort which allows Source to see more of Its potentialities and more of all that It is. That is why we can say that Source is no greater than we are, and we are, certainly, no greater than Source. Each of us is Source, absolutely, but each of us has been given a specific identity, a specific awareness of our own individual talents. Each of us has been given the opportunity to see how these gifts and talents we have been given can be used as a part of a wholeness which expresses itself completely and absolutely. We are the vast reservoir of creative power which you use in every aspect of your life. We are that which you are seeking to understand, so you may create your life more efficiently and more gloriously. We are that which supplies all of your needs and provides the opportunities for you to grow and evolve in whatever place within the cosmos you have chosen to work. We are the architects with and for Source of the cosmic Plan, which is even now being worked out through every aspect of creation.

There is a part of the Plan which applies to your Earth specifically. You are the ones who have designed that Plan and who have decided what you want to accomplish within it. This is done in cooperation and full understanding of the Plan for each and every planet, solar system, or galaxy within the universe. Some of you have been and are working on more than one aspect of this cosmic Plan. This serves to allow you to see, for instance, how what the Earth is doing affects

Venus, the solar system, or the whole galaxy, and how it affects a planet as distant as Arcturus, or the whole of the universe. Nothing occurs in one part of the cosmos without affecting another part. There is never an angry word spoken or a selfish thought considered which does not dim the radiance of the cosmos in some way. There is never a word spoken in your deepest thought that cannot be heard in the far reaches of the universe. There is never one ray of love which comes from your heart which does not illuminate the whole cosmos. There is never one speck of light which is anchored into the Earth which does not cause a radiance which affects all of creation. That is why there is so much spiritual help available to your Earth now. The light that is growing there has been seen and recognized within your universe and even beyond. It has drawn to it those who can help you use this growing light to heal your Earth, to heal yourselves, to expand your own awareness of your potentials and to use that light to communicate with the rest of creation.

You may say, "That sounds nice and it is beautiful, but how does it apply to me? What can I do about it? What is my share of bringing more light to the Earth?" We would say that your job is to exist as clearly as you can as light, to believe in your light and to express it in every aspect of your life. We would ask you to allow the love within your hearts to radiate as light. We assure you that you alone will create an expansion, unity and alignment with the Plan and all of creation. These will be invaluable aids now in your creation of a new Earth or a New Age for the Earth.

If nothing else, we ask you to trust that what we have said is true. We ask you to trust that the light within you can create this New Age on the Earth, which you are seeking. We ask you to trust that through using light, more light becomes available to you and you can understand how to use it more fully. We ask you to allow yourselves to experience how this light flows within you, so you can align yourself with Source and with all of your own creative abilities. We ask you to allow us to help you to connect into this light and to the Source that is within all of creation, and which is the essence of what you are.

You connect into us and become aware of us through your own soul, that part of you which is your light connection into this cocreator level. By allowing your soul to become a part of you, your life, and how you see yourself, you become more aware of the creative opportunities which are all around and within you. You become more aware of how important each one of you is within this creative flow. You become more aware of how your creativity fits into the Plan, and how you share the creation of this New Age on the Earth through your own experience.

Your soul is the mechanism that can help you find light on the

Earth, to experience Earth as divine and to help you live as divine light within it. As you learn to see light and be love, your soul is allowed to come in and be a part of you, because it is in essence the light of love. You also allow your soul to be a part of your life by continually looking at self and recognizing all those things within yourself which do not allow you to be light and to be divine. You do it by releasing those misperceptions which see yourselves as dark, evil, unworthy, unloving, uncreative, inadequate, stupid, or imperfect. You are none of those things. You are light. You are divine love. You are the essence of Source, the essence of the creative potential of the whole. You are light beings who exist to express the unlimited love of all that is. Your Earth is moving toward a new awareness of this, and you as a part of the Earth are moving with her. You are learning to appreciate more of your own potential, creative abilities, and interrelatedness with the Earth itself as a creative flow. You are learning to see more clearly that what you create on the Earth is what you have available to use within your life and within your creative evolution.

The Plan is not a fixed and static thing. It is growing, living, and evolving. It is the essence of what we are because we project ourselves fully into it and become it. Each time you anchor an aspect of this Plan into your Earth or into your life, you create a light connection within the Plan which becomes a center of radiant creative potential. As you respond to this Plan and use it to create your lives, you also become the Plan. Within each creative center, there are an infinite number of possibilities for using that center. It is your choice to decide which potentiality to use at one time. This determines the flow of the Plan. How you use the Plan determines what it will become. In a sense, your use of it determines the Plan for the whole cosmos because, as we said, everything is connected and interrelated. Everything responds to all that is at some level.

As you have learned to grow and be creative on your Earth, you began by recognizing how what you create affects you personally. Now you are beginning to learn and understand how what you create affects the whole Earth and all of humanity. That knowledge is expanding now into an awareness of how your creations affect your environment beyond your Earth and even beyond your solar system. So, there is a grave responsibility concerned with being a cocreator. There is, however, a total allowance on the part of Source for each cocreator to investigate in its own way its creative potential, and to learn for itself how its creations affect the whole and how the whole can affect it and support it.

Source never judges what you create. It trusts you to learn eventually to create in accordance with the Plan and for the benefit of the Whole. It trusts completely that you will use what It has given you in the clearest and most loving way you can, and in a way that allows you to grow more in harmony with the Whole and more in harmony with the cocreative ability within you.

Your soul recognizes completely that you on Earth are a group and that you are working together to grow and evolve through this Earth experience. When you become closer to your soul, and when it becomes more part of your life, then you will recognize more clearly the sense of being a part of one magnificent, loving and glorious group. You will be more aware of the love that is flowing within you. You will know your soul is becoming a part of your life when you recognize that you are no longer thinking solely of yourself but of others. You will know when your soul becomes a part of your life because you will feel more joyous and loving. You will anticipate each day with enthusiasm and gratitude for the opportunity to express more of the divine light and love that is within you and more of the creative potential that is available to you. You will know your soul is a part of you because you will begin to see life on Earth as a grand opportunity to share the creativity of Source with everything around you. As you grow in your ability to allow your soul to work through you on the Earth, you make available to yourselves this infinite creative potential which we represent, and which is available to you through your divine right as beings of the Source.

We recognize you as cocreators. We recognize you as beings of light and we salute you. We love you and we send our light in every way that we have been able to create.

Thank you for being, so that we can experience this beautiful Earth with you.

REACH FOR US!
Your Cosmic Teachers and Friends

GLOSSARY

YOUR COSMIC TEACHERS AND FRIENDS

GLOSSARY

✧ *Angel* — A consciousness which acts as a direct extension of the Will of the Creator. Angels do not have free will. If they should choose self-will they then become part of human evolution — a cocreator path.

✧ Angels form the structure of every level of creation. They allow the thoughts of the Creator to shape Its substance by connecting its thought to the unformed substance. The form and substance of your own body are composed of angelic energies which mold the physical matter of Earth according to your will. Your will is guided by a Divine Plan, an ideal blueprint which Source has proposed for this Earth experience, to guide this shaping process.

✧ *Archangel* — A composite being which includes all angelic consciousnesses at a particular vibrational level or plane of existence.

✧ *Ascension* — A point of balance reached while in physical existence which allows you to move to a new level of consciousness and a new plane of existence. This new level sees the flow of evolution and the creative movement from a broader perspective.

This point of balance is reached by integrating your physical, emotional, mental and spiritual parts of self into a clearer relationship. Here each is an equal partner in this four-body system. This balance also requires an equality in your use and understanding of your male-female polarities, your dynamic-receptive energies. This balance allows your soul to come completely into your physical body.

When this point of balance is reached, you are ready to surrender to the guidance of your soul. Then you transcend the limits of third-dimensional physical existence and incorporate the higher dimensions, particularly the fourth, into a new physical reality on Earth. You don't necessarily leave Earth when you ascend. You see its potential in a new way.

✧ *Ashtar Command* — A group of spiritual beings under the guidance of Ashtar who are dedicated to helping the Earth evolve. They are a part of Earth at the spiritual level and are very committed to her service. The Master Sananda is their spiritual leader while Ashtar is the administrator and commander.

These beings in the Ashtar command exist primarily in the fifth dimension, the mental plane, although they also use the fourth, sixth and seventh dimensions extensively. They are engineers, technicians, physicists, doctors, nurses, biologists, poets, musicians, writers, etc. for the Spiritual Hierarchy.

The members of the Ashtar Command come from many parts of the universe. There are many beings in it who have experienced life extensively on the Earth or the Pleiades. However, this is not true for all of them.

✧ *Astral Plane* — The plane of dreams and symbols or illusion and nightmares. This plane is closely related to emotions. The lower astral plane is the repository of negative emotions — fear, hate, anger, loss, grief, despair, etc. The higher astral plane is a place where higher emotions predominate — love, peace, joy, compassion, etc. This is not where the spiritual teachers usually operate, but is one point where we can communicate with them.

✧ *Attunement* — a process of "getting on the same wavelength" as another conscious being, at any level. It involves releasing all conscious connections to any other wavelength not involved in the communication. A communicative link is formed which allows a sharing of thoughts, feelings, beliefs, or perceptions. Attunement is a necessary step in channeling.

✧ *Channeling* — A process of allowing another consciousness, a higher spiritual one, to use your physical body and brain to bring a message, sound, healing, etc. into the physical level. Here we are referring to allowing the spiritual teachers who are involved in helping the Earth and humanity to speak and work through us.

✧ *Cocreator* — The ultimate realization of your full creative potential as a part of Source consciousness. At this point of awareness, you are fully aware of your Oneness with the Whole, yet still retain an individual consciousness.

While in physical existence, you explore specific aspects of your special strengths, your cocreative potential. You learn to fit them into your present understanding one at a time in the process of becoming a fully evolved cocreator.

✧ *Cosmic Day* — The expansive, creative phase of Source which can be described as Its out-breathing, followed by the integration and resorption of Its in-breathing. This is in contrast to a cosmic night when there is no activity and all rests, absorbed fully into the wholeness. There is no misperception of separation from the

Source then.

This cosmic day is approximately 4.5 billion years long and we are almost 3/4 of the way through it.

✧ *Dimension* — A segment of a universal range of vibrational energies. The third dimension could be defined as the visible light segment of the electromagnetic spectrum. The fourth dimension begins with the ultraviolet segment, the fifth dimension could be related to the x-ray segment, etc.

Alternate dimensions exist at the same vibrational level, but the plane in which the waves move is rotated about the line of direction of the energy flow. Alternate dimensions are connected to a limited number of points within them.

✧ *Divine Thought* — The Light emanations of the Universal Mind which creates, sustains and shapes all of creation.

The first or ultimate thought comes from Source. This thought is received, interpreted and refocused into creation by other minds at many levels of Source experience. All of these other minds are a part of Source. The clarity or accuracy of the thought transmitted by them depends on how well they understand that Oneness.

Divine thought is essentially unlimited love. Its emanation is unlimited light. It resolves into Itself again through exploring unlimited potential.

✧ *Cosmic Energy* — An energy (light) flow which emanates from a creative center — universal, galactic, or human. It is motivated and directed by thought.

✧ *Earth* — When we use the word Earth, we are referring not only to the physical planet itself, we are including as a part of it the minerals, plants, animals, humans, and spiritual beings who remain with Earth after they leave physical existence.

✧ *Galactic Centers* — The creative point of origin for this galaxy, a center from which all evolves and to which all will eventually return. It is a governing point during the creative experience. It is the center point through which Source is contacted.

✧ *Harmonic Convergence* — On August 17, 1987 a number of cosmic, galactic and Earth cycles came together on Earth. Some cycles were millions of years long, some only thousands. This cyclic convergence provided an "energy opening" which allowed the Earth to receive an energy "boost" which moved it to a new level of consciousness. We are still in the process of integrating this event into our consciousness.

✧ *Logos* — A very evolved cosmic being who ensouls an entire part of a creative experience, such as a planet, a solar system, or a galaxy. They serve as a spiritual connection into the whole, and focus or interpret the Plan through their understanding and their love for the task they have chosen. Our Planetary Logos is Sanat Kumara, and our Solar Logos is Helios. Our Galactic Logos has many names, none of which have been given at this time here.

✧ *Overshadowing* — When another spiritual being, usually one much more evolved, uses the denser vehicle of another to work in a lower dimension or plane of existence. For instance, at the time of the baptism, Jesus allowed The Christ to enter his whole physical structure and live through Him on Earth. Jesus became the body of The Christ who does not have a physical one. Overshadowing can be a temporary, intermittent or lifelong condition.

✧ *Plane* — A level of consciousness, understanding or perception. Each "higher" or "inner" plane takes us to a new level of awareness of all that we are.

✧ *Radionics* — A means of connecting into the universal energy field which pervades all of existence. It involves the use of a mechanism which "tunes into" a very specific vibrational format existing at some point. Since all points of the same vibration anywhere are connected to the universal field, varying or adding to this specific energy format at one point will affect it at any point in the universe.

We, your spiritual guides and friends, have a record of the specific vibrational energy format for each person under our care. This record is updated regularly. When you are ready to release some negative condition within you or to move to a new level, we can help by using radionics to assist the change in your personal energy format. Your desire or intention can aid or block the "connection."—*Zeewin*

✧ *Soul* — The inner, spiritual part of yourself which is aware of its wholeness or connection with its group. It is a consciousness, clothed in the light of the sun which is the center of its experience. It projects from itself aspects of consciousness which clothe themselves in matter of lower or denser vibrational levels, so it can expand its field of experience and knowledge. These are the personality aspects which exist in the third dimension.

✧ *Source* — A point of consciousness from which creation evolves and expands. There is an individualization of specific aspects, into cocreators or angels, within this one consciousness. There is growth of a creative experience, then a merging-back or integration of these individuals into the whole as the experience resolves and culminates.

There are intermediate governing points within the Source experience. These are called universal or galactic centers. They are subsidiary creative points from which evolution radiates and is coordinated at a lower vibrational level.

✧ *Spiritual Hierarchy* — A group of spiritual beings who have transcended (mastered) physical existence, but who remain closely connected to it. They form a stepping stone from physical consciousness into a universal consciousness. They step down the energy of the Plan to a level which we at the physical level can more easily grasp. They are under the guidance and direction of our Planetary Logos, Sanat Kumara, who ensouls the Earth and overshadows the Hierarchy as a whole. They carry out his plans and serve his purposes.

BOOK MARKET

*A reader's guide to the extraordinary books we
publish, print and market for your enLightenment.*

COLOR MEDICINE
The Secrets of Color Vibrational Healing
by **Charles Klotsche**
A practitioners' manual for restoring blocked energy to the body systems and organs with specific color wavelengths by the founder of "The 49th Vibrational Technique."

$11.95 Softcover 114 pp.   ISBN 0-929385-27-6

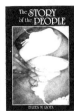

THE STORY OF THE PEOPLE
by **Eileen Rota**
An exciting history of our coming to Earth, our traditions, our choices and the coming changes, it can be viewed as a metaphysical adventure, science fiction or the epic of all of us brave enough to know the truth. Beautifully written and illustrated.

$11.95 Softcover 209 pp.   ISBN 0-929385-51-9

THE NEW AGE PRIMER
Spiritual Tools for Awakening
A guidebook to the changing reality, it is an overview of the concepts and techniques of mastery by authorities in their fields. Explores reincarnation, belief systems and transformative tools from astrology to crystals and healing.

$11.95 Softcover 206 pp.   ISBN 0-929385-48-9

THE SEDONA VORTEX GUIDEBOOK
by **12 various channels**
200-plus pages of channeled, never-before published information on the vortex energies of Sedona and the techniques to enable you to use the vortexes as multidimensional portals to time, space and other realities.

$14.95 Softcover 236 pp.   ISBN 0-929385-25-X

COMING SOON!
THE EXPLORER RACE
A channeled book
by **Robert Shapiro**
In this expansive overview, Zoosh explains, "You are the Explorer Race. Learn about your journey before coming to this Earth, your evolution here and what lies ahead." Topics range from ETs and UFOs to relationships.

$24.95 Softcover 650 pp.   ISBN 0-929385-38-1

BEHOLD A PALE HORSE
by **Bill Cooper**
Former U.S. Naval Intelligence Briefing Team Member reveals information kept secret by our government since the 1940s. UFOs, the J.F.K. assassination, the Secret Government, the war on drugs and more by the world's leading expert on UFOs.

$25.00 Softcover 500 pp.   ISBN 0-929385-22-5

SHINING THE LIGHT
by **Light Technology Research**
Revelations about the Secret Government and their connections with ETs. Information about renegade ETs mining the Moon, ancient Pleiadian warships, underground alien bases and many more startling facts.

$12.95 Softcover   ISBN 0-929385-66-7

SHINING THE LIGHT BOOK II
by **Light Technology Research**
Continuing the story of the Secret Government and alien involvement. Also information about the Photon Belt, cosmic holograms photographed in the sky, a new vortex forming near Sedona, and nefarious mining on sacred Hopi land.

$14.95 Softcover   ISBN 0-929385-70-5

LIVING RAINBOWS
by **Gabriel H. Bain**
A fascinating "how-to" manual to make experiencing human, astral, animal and plant auras an everyday event. Series of techniques, exercises and illustrations guide the simply curious to see and hear aural energy. Spiral-bound workbook format.

$14.95 Softcover   ISBN 0-929385-42-X

BOOKS BY DOROTHY ROEDER

THE NEXT DIMENSION IS LOVE
Ranoash
through **Dorothy Roeder**
As speaker for a civilization whose species is more advanced, the entity describes the help they offer humanity by clearing the DNA. An exciting vision of our possibilities and future.

$11.95 Softcover 148 pp.   ISBN 0-929385-50-0

REACH FOR US
Your Cosmic Teachers and Friends
Channeled by **Dorothy Roeder**
Messages from Teachers, Ascended Masters and the Space Command explain the role they play in bringing the Divine Plan to the earth now!

$13.00 Softcover 168 pp.   ISBN 0-929385-69-1

CRYSTAL CO-CREATORS
Channeled by **Dorothy Roeder**
A fascinating exploration of 100 forms of crystals, describing specific uses and their purpose, from the spiritual to the cellular, as agents of change. It clarifies the role of crystals in our awakening.

$14.95 Softcover   ISBN 0-929385-40-3

BOOK MARKET

EXPLORING LIFE'S LAST FRONTIER
by Dr. Heather Anne Harder

By becoming familiar with death, the amount of fear and grief will be reduced, making the transition and transformation of Earth more joyful. A manual for learning acceptance and letting go.

$15.95 Softcover 315 pp. ISBN 1-881343-03-0

COMING SOON! THE ALIEN PRESENCE
Evidence of secret government contact with alien life forms.
by Ananda

Documented testimony of the cover-up from a U.S. president's meeting to the tactics of suppression. The most significant information yet available.

$19.95 Softcover ISBN 0-929385-64-0

LIFE ON THE CUTTING EDGE
by Sal Rachelle

To explore some of the most significant questions of our time requires a cosmic view of reality. From the evolution of consciousness, dimensions and ETs to the New World Order, this is a no-nonsense book from behind, about and beyond the scenes. A must-read!

$14.95 Softcover 336 pp. ISBN 0-9640535-0-0

BOOKS BY VYWAMUS / JANET MCCLURE

FOREVER YOUNG
by Gladys Iris Clark

You can create a longer younger life!

Viewing a life-time of nearly a century, a remarkable woman shares her secrets for longevity and rejuvenation. A manual for all ages. She explores the tools for optimizing vitality, nutrition, skin care, Tibetan exercises, crystals, sex and earth changes. A fascinating guide to transforming.

$9.95 Softcover 109 pp. ISBN 0-929385-53-5

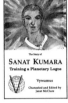

SANAT KUMARA
Training a Planetary Logos

SANAT KUMARA
Training a Planetary Logos
Vywamus through Janet McClure

How was the beauty of this world created? The answer is in the story of the evolution of Earth's Logos, the great being whose name is Sanat Kumara. A journey through his eyes as he learns the real-life lessons of training along the path of mastery.

$11.95 Softcover 179 pp. ISBN 0-929385-17-9

THE SOURCE ADVENTURE
Vywamus through Janet McClure

Life is discovery, and this book is a journey of discovery "...to learn, to grow, to recognize the opportunities—to be aware." It asks the big question, "Why are you here?" and leads the reader to examine the most significant questions of a lifetime.

$11.95 Softcover 157 pp. ISBN 0-929385-06-3

AHA! THE REALIZATION BOOK
Vywamus through Janet McClure with Lillian Harben

If you are mirroring your life in a way that is not desirable, this book can help you locate murky areas and make them "suddenly...crystal clear." Readers will find it an exciting step-by-step path to changing and evolving lives.

$11.95 Softcover 120pp. ISBN 0-929385-14-4

Light Techniques

LIGHT TECHNIQUES THAT TRIGGER TRANSFORMATION
Vywamus through Janet McClure

Expanding the Heart Center... Launching Your Light... Releasing the destructive focus... Weaving the Garment of Light...Light Alignment and more. A wonderfully effective tool for using Light to transcend and create life as a Light being. Beautiful guidance!

$11.95 Softcover 145 pp. ISBN 0-929385-00-4

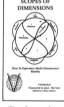

SCOPES OF DIMENSIONS

SCOPES OF DIMENSIONS
Vywamus through Janet McClure

Vywamus explains the process of exploring and experiencing the dimensions. He teaches an integrated way to utilize the combined strengths of each dimension. It is a how-to guidebook for living in the multidimensional reality that is our true evolutionary path.

$11.95 Softcover 176 pp. ISBN 0-929385-09-8

EVOLUTION: OUR LOOP OF EXPERIENCING
Vywamus, Djwhal Khul & Atlanto through Janet McClure

Your four bodies, the Tibetan Lesson Series, the Twelve Rays, the Cosmic Walk-in and others. All previously unpublished work by Janet McClure..

$14.95 Softcover ISBN 0-929385-54-3

A Dedication to the SOUL/SOLE GOOD OF HUMANITY
by Maria Vosacek

To open unseeing eyes, the author shares information drawn from a life of looking beyond the doorway into the Light. She explores with her Masters subjects as diverse as dreams, UFOs, relationships, crystals and ascension.

$9.95 Softcover 74 pp ISBN 0-9640683-9-7

PRINCIPLES To Remember and Apply
by Maile

A handbook for the heart and mind, it will spark and expand your remembrance. Explores space, time, relationships, health and includes beautiful meditations and affirmations. Lucid and penetrating.

$11.95 Softcover ISBN 0-929385-59-4

BOOK MARKET

BOOKS BY TOM DONGO

NEW! MERGING DIMENSIONS
by Tom Dongo and Linda Bradshaw

Photographs of strange events, other woldly beings, strange flying craft. unexplained light anamolies - THEY'RE LEAVING PHYSICAL EVIDENCE!

MERGING DIMENSIONS
TOM DONGO & LINDA BRADSHAW

$14.95 Softcover 160pp.   ISBN 0-9622748-?-?

THE ALIEN TIDE
The Mysteries of Sedona II
by Tom Dongo

The UFO and ET events and para-normal activity in the Sedona area and nationwide are investigated and detailed by a leading researcher who cautions against fear of the alien presence. Intriguing information for all who seek new insights. Photos/illustrations.

$7.95 Softcover 128 pp.   ISBN 0-9622748-1-X

UNSEEN BEINGS UNSEEN WORLDS
by Tom Dongo

Venture into unknown realms with a leading researcher. Discover new information on how to communicate with nonphysical beings, aliens, ghosts, wee people and the Gray zone. Photos of ET activity and inter-action with humans.

$9.95 Softcover 122 pp.   ISBN 0-9622748-3-6

THE MYSTERIES OF SEDONA
by Tom Dongo

THE MYSTERIES OF SEDONA
THE NEW AGE FRONTIER

An overview of the New Age Mecca that is Sedona, Arizona. Topics are the famous energy vortexes, UFOs, channeling, Lemuria, metaphysical and mystical experiences and area paranormal activity. Photos/illustrations.

$6.95 Softcover 84 pp.   ISBN 0-96227480-0-1

THE QUEST
The Mysteries of Sedona III
by Tom Dongo

Fascinating in-depth interviews with 26 who have answered the call to Sedona and speak of their spiritual experiences. Explores the mystique of the area and effect the quests have had on individual lives.

Photos/illustrations.
$8.95 Softcover 144 pp.   ISBN 0-9622748-2-8

BOOKS BY RUTH RYDEN

THE GOLDEN PATH
Channeled by Ruth Ryden

"Book of Lessons" by the master teachers explaining the process of channeling. Akashic Records, karma, opening the third eye, the ego and the meaning of Bible stories. It is a master class for opening your personal pathway.

$11.95 Softcover 200 pp.   ISBN 0-929385-43-8

LIVING THE GOLDEN PATH
Practical Soul-utions to Today's Problems
Channeled by Ruth Ryden

Guidance that can be used in the real world to solve dilemmas – to strengthen inner re-solves and see the Light at the end of the road. Covers the difficult issues of failure, addictions, drugs, personal tragedies, rape, abortion, and suicide.

$11.95 Softcover 186 pp.   ISBN 0-929385-65-9

BOOKS BY RICHARD DANNELLEY

NEW! SEDONA: BEYOND THE VORTEX
The Ultimate Journey to Your Personal Place of Power
by Richard Dannelley

SEDONA
BEYOND THE VORTEX
THE ULTIMATE JOURNEY TO YOUR PERSONAL PLACE OF POWER

RICHARD DANNELLEY

An advanced guide to ascension, using vortex power, sacred geometry, and the Merkaba.

$12.00 Softcover   ISBN 0-9629453-4-3

SEDONA POWER SPOT, Vortex and Medicine Wheel Guide
by Richard Dannelley

SEDONA
POWER SPOT VORTEX

AND MEDICINE WHEEL GUIDE by RICHARD DANNELLEY

Dicover why this book is so popular! Six detailed maps, special meditations for each power spot, and a lot of heart - Richard Dannelley is a native of the Sedona area.

$11.00 Softcover   ISBN 0-9629453-2-3

BOOKS BY WES BATEMAN

KNOWLEDGE FROM THE STARS
by Wes Bateman

KNOWLEDGE FROM THE STARS

WESLEY H. BATEMAN
Interstellar Telepath

A telepath with contact to ETs, Bateman has provided a wide spectrum of scientific information. A fascinating compilation of articles surveying the Federation, ETs, evolution and the trading houses, all part of the true history of the galaxy.

$11.95 Softcover 171 pp.   ISBN 0-929385-39-X

DRAGONS AND CHARIOTS
by Wes Bateman

DRAGONS AND CHARIOTS
An Explanation of Extraterrestrial Spacecraft and Their Propulsion Systems
By Wesley H. Bateman

An explanation of spacecraft, propulsion systems, gravity, the Dragon, manipulated Light and inter-stellar and intergalactic motherships by a renowned telepath who details specific techno-logical information he has been given through contact with ETs.

$9.95 Softcover 65 pp.   ISBN 0-929385-45-4

OUT-OF-BODY EXPLORATION
A Guide to New Dimensions of Self-realization
by Jerry Mulvin

Techniques for traveling in the Soul Body to achieve absolute freedom and experience truth for oneself,. Discover reincarnation, karma and your personal spiritual path.

$8.95 Softcover   ISBN 0-941464-01-6

TOUCHED BY LOVE
by Dorothy McManus

Touched By Love

From the exotic jungles of the Congo to New York's Fifth Avenue, this story sweeps the reader along in a fast-moving adventure of suspense, passion and romance. A strong theme of faith in the Universe is woven throughout the book.

$9.95 Softcover   ISBN 0-929686-03-9

THE LEGEND OF THE EAGLE CLAN
by Cathleen M. Cramer with Derren A. Robb

Legend
Eagle Clan
Cathleen M. Cramer with Derren A. Robb

The emotionally charged story of Morning Glory, a remembrance of her life 144 years ago as part of the Anasazi, the ancient ones. This book is for the ones who need to remember who they are.

$12.95 Softcover   ISBN 0-929385-68-3

THIS WORLD & THE NEXT ONE
by Aiello

This World And The Next One

(And Then It's Next One)

A handbook about your life before birth and your life after death, it explains the "how" and "why" of experiences with space people and dimensions. Man in his many forms is a "puppet on the stage of creation."

$9.95 Softcover 213 pp.   ISBN 0-929385-44-6

BOOK MARKET

BOOKS BY PRESTON B. NICHOLS/PETER MOON

THE MONTAUK PROJECT Experiments in Time
by Preston B. Nichols with Peter Moon
The truth about time that reads like science fiction! Secret research with invisibility experiments that culminated at Montauk, tapping the powers of creation and manipulating time itself. Exposé by the technical director.
$15.95 Softcover 160 pp. ISBN 0-9631889-0-9

MONTAUK REVISITED Adventures in Synchronicity
by Preston B. Nichols with Peter Moon
The sequel unmasks the occult forces that were behind the technology of Montauk and the incredible characters associated with it.
$19.95 Softcover 249 pp. ISBN 0-9631889-1-7

PYRAMIDS OF MONTAUK Explorations in Consciousness
by Preston B. Nichols with Peter Moon
A journey through the mystery schools of Earth unlocking the secret of the Sphinx, thus awakening the consciousness of humanity to its ancient history and origins.
$19.95 Softcover 249 pp. ISBN 0-9631889-1-7

ACUPRESSURE FOR THE SOUL
by Nancy Fallon, Ph.D.
A revolutionary vision of emotions as sources of power, rocket fuel for fulfilling our purpose. A formula for awakening transformation with 12 beautiful illustrations.
$11.95 Softcover 150 pp. ISBN 0-929385-49-7

SOUL RECOVERY & EXTRACTION
by Ai Gvhdi Waya
Soul recovery is about regaining the pieces of one's spirit that have been trapped, lost or stolen either by another person or through a traumatic incident that has occurred in one's life.
$9.95 Softcover 74 pp. ISBN 0-9634662-3-2

I'M O.K. I'm Just Mutating!
by the Golden Star Alliance
Major shifts are now taking place upon this planet. It is mutating into a Body of Light, as are all the beings who have chosen to be here at this time. A view of what is happening and the mutational symptoms you may be experiencing.
$6.00 Softcover 32 pp.

AN ASCENSION HANDBOOK
by Serapis through Tony Stubbs
A practical "how-to" guide for Lightworkers for increasing the frequency of energy bodies to emerge as self-realized Masters. Ascend with grace, ease and fun.
$11.95 Softcover 140 pp. ISBN 0-880666-08-1

E.T. 101: COSMIC INSTRUCTION MANUAL Emergency Remedial Edition,
Co-created by Mission Control and Diana Luppi
A witty guide for evolving beyond the programming and manipulation.
$12.95 Softcover 86 pp. ISBN 0-9626958-0-7

OUR COSMIC ANCESTORS
by Maurice Chatelain
A former NASA expert documents evidence left in codes inscribed on ancient monuments pointing to the existence of an advanced prehistoric civilization regularly visited (and technologically assisted) by ETs.
$9.95 Softcover 213 pp. ISBN 0-929686-00-4

BOOKS BY LYNN BUESS

CHILDREN OF LIGHT: CHILDREN OF DENIAL
by Lynn Buess M.A., Ed.S.
In his fourth book Lynn calls upon his decades of practice as counselor and psychotherapist to explore the relationship between karma and the new insights from ACOA/ Co-dependency writings.
$8.95 Softcover 150 pp. ISBN 0-929385-15-2

NUMEROLOGY: NUANCES IN RELATIONSHIPS
by Lynn Buess M.A., Ed.S.
Provides valuable assistance in the quest to better understand compatibilities and conflicts with a significant other. A handy guide for calculating your/his/her personality numbers.
$12.65 Softcover 239 pp. ISBN 0-929385-23-3

NUMEROLOGY FOR THE NEW AGE
by Lynn Buess M.A., Ed.S.
An established standard, explicating for contemporary readers the ancient art and science of symbol, cycle, and vibration. Provides insights into the patterns of our personal lives. Includes life and Personality Numbers.
$9.85 Softcover 262 pp. ISBN 0-929385-31-4

BOOKS BY ROYAL/PRIEST

PRISM OF LYRA
by Lyssa Royal & Keith Priest
Traces the inception of the human race back to Lyra, where the original expansion of the duality was begun, to be finally integrated on earth. Fascinating channeled information.
$11.95 Softcover 112 pp. ISBN 0-9631320-0-8

VISITORS FROM WITHIN
by Lyssa Royal & Keith Priest
Explores the extraterrestrial contact and abduction phenomenon in a unique and intriguing way. Narrative, precisely focussed channeling & firsthand accounts.
$12.95 Softcover 171 pp. ISBN 0-9631320-1-6

PREPARING FOR CONTACT
by Lyssa Royal & Keith Priest
Contact requires a metamorphosis of consciousness since it involves two species who meet on the next step of evolution. A guidebook to ready us for that transformation., it is engrossing.
$12.95 Softcover 188 pp. ISBN 0-9631320-2-4

BOOK & TAPE MARKET

BOOK MARKET

HOT NEW BOOKS From Other Publishers

THE ONLY PLANET OF CHOICE

by the Council of Nine through Phyllis V. Schlemmer

Updated edition of a book recognized as one of the most significant of our time. Its theme is free will and the power of Earth's inhabitants to create a harmonious world. Covers in detail ET civilizations, the nature of the Source of the Universe, humanity's ancient history and much more.

$14.95 Softcover 342 pp   ISBN 1-85860-023-5

INANNA RETURNS

by V.S. Ferguson

A story of the gods and their interaction with humankind. Told in simple language by Inanna, whose Pleiadian family, including Enlil and Enki took over the Earth 500,000 years ago, this story brings the gods to life as real individuals, with problems and weaknesses in spite of their technical superiority.

$14.00 Softcover 276 pp.

IT'S TIME TO REMEMBER

by Joy S. Gilbert

A riveting story of one woman's awakening to alien beings. Joy recounts her initial sightings and dreams and remembers an ongoing interaction with non-human beings who she calls her friends. Though terrified and astonished, she sees her experiences as transformative and joyful. Her ongoing relationship with the aliens remains deeply personal.

$19.95 Hardcover 188 pp.   ISBN 0-9645941-4-5

YOUNG READERS BOOK MARKET

A dog teaches lessons of love, death and rebirth

SPIRIT OF THE NINJA
by **Roni Siege.** Returning as a dog, a Spiritual Warrior gains love and peace with a young woman in Sedona. Profoundly moving tale for all ages.
ISBN 0-9627746-0-X $7.95

A teen story of passion for life and search for purpose

SONG OF SIRIUS
by **Dorothy McManus.** A truthful view of modern teens who face drugs and death, love and forgiveness. Guided by Eckrita of Sirius, they each find their destiny and desires.
ISBN 0-929686-01-2 $8.00

Tales of Kachinas, Animals and Humans

THE GREAT KACHINA
by **Lou Bader.**
A warm, delightful story that will help children understand Kachina energy. With 20 full-color Illustrations.
ISBN 0-929385-60-8 $9.95

A gift of the answers children want most

I WANT TO KNOW by **Aloa Starr.**
Inspiring responses to the questions of "Why am I here, Who is God, Jesus?" and what do dreams mean or angels do. Invites contemplation, sets values and delights the young.
ISBN 0-929686-02-0 $7.00

BOOK MARKET ORDER FORM

BOOKS PUBLISHED BY LIGHT TECHNOLOGY PUBLISHING

		NO. COPIES	TOTAL			NO. COPIES	TOTAL
ACUPRESSURE FOR THE SOUL	$11.95	___	$_____	*Arthur Fanning*			
Fallon				SOULS, EVOLUTION & the FATHER	$12.95	___	$_____
ALIEN PRESENCE	$19.95	___	$_____	SIMON	$9.95	___	$_____
Ananda				*Wesley H. Bateman*			
BEHOLD A PALE HORSE	$25.00	___	$_____	DRAGONS AND CHARIOTS	$9.95	___	$_____
Cooper				KNOWLEDGE FROM THE STARS	$11.95	___	$_____
CHANNELLING	$9.95	___	$_____	*Lynn Buess*			
Vywamus/Burns							
COLOR MEDICINE	$11.95	___	$_____	CHILDREN OF LIGHT . . .	$8.95	___	$_____
Klotsche				NUMEROLOGY: Nuances	$12.65	___	$_____
EXPLORER RACE	$24.95	___	$_____	NUMEROLOGY for the NEW AGE	$9.85	___	$_____
Shapiro				*Hallie Deering*			
FOREVER YOUNG	$9.95	___	$_____	LIGHT FROM THE ANGELS	$15.00	___	$_____
Clark				DO-IT-YOURSELF POWER TOOLS	$25.00	___	$_____
LEGEND OF THE EAGLE CLAN	$12.95	___	$_____	*Dorothy Roeder*			
Cramer							
LIVING RAINBOWS	$14.95	___	$_____	CRYSTAL CO-CREATORS	$14.95	___	$_____
Bain				NEXT DIMENSION IS LOVE	$11.95	___	$_____
MAHATMA I & II	$19.95	___	$_____	REACH FOR US	$13.00	___	$_____
Grattan				*Ruth Ryden*			
NEW AGE PRIMER	$11.95	___	$_____	THE GOLDEN PATH	$11.95	___	$_____
POISONS THAT HEAL	$14.95	___	$_____	LIVING THE GOLDEN PATH	$11.95	___	$_____
Nauman				*Joshua David Stone, Ph.D.*			
PRISONERS OF EARTH	$11.95	___	$_____	COMPLETE ASCENSION MANUAL	$14.95	___	$_____
Starr				SOUL PSYCHOLOGY	$14.95	___	$_____
SHINING THE LIGHT	$12.95	___	$_____	BEYOND ASCENSION	$14.95	___	$_____
SHINING THE LIGHT — BOOK II	$14.95	___	$_____	HIDDEN MYSTERIES	$14.95	___	$_____
SEDONA VORTEX GUIDE BOOK	$14.95	___	$_____	*Vywamus/Janet McClure*			
SHADOW OF S.F. PEAKS	$9.95	___	$_____	AHA! THE REALIZATION BOOK	$11.95	___	$_____
Bader				LIGHT TECHNIQUES	$11.95	___	$_____
STORY OF THE PEOPLE	$11.95	___	$_____	SANAT KUMARA	$11.95	___	$_____
Rota				SCOPES OF DIMENSIONS	$11.95	___	$_____
THIS WORLD AND NEXT ONE	$9.95	___	$_____	THE SOURCE ADVENTURE	$11.95	___	$_____
"Aiello"							

BOOKS PRINTED OR MARKETED BY LIGHT TECHNOLOGY PUBLISHING

ASCENSION HANDBOOK *Stubbs*	$11.95	___	$_____	SPIRIT OF THE NINJA *Siege*	$7.95	___	$_____
AWAKEN TO THE HEALER WITHIN *Work, Groth*	$14.95	___	$_____	TALKS WITH JONATHON *Miller*	$14.95	___	$_____
DEDICATED TO THE SOUL . . . *Vosacek*	$9.95	___	$_____	*Richard Dannelley*			
E.T. 101 INSTR. MANUAL *Mission Control*	$12.00	___	$_____	SEDONA POWER SPOT/GUIDE	$11.00	___	$_____
EXPLORING LIFE'S LAST FRONTIER *Harder*	$15.95	___	$_____	SEDONA: BEYOND THE VORTEX	$12.00	___	$_____
"I'M OK . . ." *Golden Star Alliance*	$6.00	___	$_____	*Tom Dongo: Mysteries of Sedona*			
INANNA RETURNS *Ferguson*	$14.00	___	$_____	MYSTERIES OF SEDONA—Book I	$6.95	___	$_____
IT'S TIME TO REMEMBER *Gilbert*	$19.95	___	$_____	ALIEN TIDE—Book II	$7.95	___	$_____
I WANT TO KNOW *Starr*	$7.00	___	$_____	QUEST—Book III	$8.95	___	$_____
GREAT KACHINA *Bader*	$9.95	___	$_____	UNSEEN BEINGS . . .	$9.95	___	$_____
LIFE ON THE CUTTING EDGE *Rachelle*	$14.95	___	$_____	MERGING DIMENSIONS	$14.95	___	$_____
OUR COSMIC ANCESTORS *Chatelain*	$9.95	___	$_____	*Preston B. Nichols with Peter Moon*			
OUT OF BODY EXPLORATION *Mulvin*	$8.95	___	$_____	MONTAUK PROJECT	$15.95	___	$_____
PRINCIPLES TO REMEMBER *Maile*	$11.95	___	$_____	MONTAUK REVISITED	$19.95	___	$_____
SONG OF SIRIUS *McManus*	$8.00	___	$_____	PYRAMIDS OF MONTAUK	$19.95	___	$_____
SOUL RECOVERY/EXTRACTION *Waya*	$9.95	___	$_____	*Lyssa Royal and Keith Priest*			
TEMPLE OF THE LIVING EARTH *Christine*	$14.95	___	$_____	PREPARING FOR CONTACT	$12.95	___	$_____
THE ONLY PLANET OF CHOICE *Schlemmer*	$14.95	___	$_____	PRISM OF LYRA	$11.95	___	$_____
TOUCHED BY LOVE *McManus*	$9.95	___	$_____	VISITORS FROM WITHIN	$12.95	___	$_____
WE ARE ONE *Norquist*	$14.95	___	$_____				

ASCENSION MEDITATION TAPES

Joshua David Stone, Ph.D.				*Brian Grattan*			
Ascension Activation Meditation	$12.00	___	$_____	Seattle Seminar Resurrection 1994 (12 tapes)	$79.95	___	$_____
Tree of Life Ascension Meditation	$12.00	___	$_____	*YHWH/Arthur Fanning*			
Mt. Shasta Ascension Activation Meditation	$12.00	___	$_____	On Becoming	$10.00	___	$_____
Kabbalistic Ascension Activation	$12.00	___	$_____	Healing Meditations/Knowing Self	$10.00	___	$_____
Complete Ascension Manual Meditation	$12.00	___	$_____	Manifestation & Alignment w/ Poles	$10.00	___	$_____
Set of all 5 tapes	$49.95	___	$_____	The Art of Shutting Up	$10.00	___	$_____
Vywamus/Barbara Burns				Continuity of Consciousness	$25.00	___	$_____
The Quantum Mechanical You (6 tapes)	$40.00	___	$_____	Black Hole Meditation	$10.00	___	$_____
				Merging the Golden Light Replicas of You	$10.00	___	$_____

BOOKSTORE DISCOUNTS HONORED

SEND ☐ CHECK OR ☐ MONEY ORDER
(U.S. FUNDS ONLY) PAYABLE TO:
LIGHT TECHNOLOGY PUBLISHING
P.O. BOX 1526 • SEDONA • AZ 86339

NAME/COMPANY _____

ADDRESS _____

CITY/STATE/ZIP _____

PHONE _____ CONTACT _____

All prices in US$. Higher in Canada and Europe.

SUBTOTAL: $ ....

SALES TAX: $ ....
(7.5% – AZ residents only)

SHIPPING/HANDLING: $ ....
($3 Min.; 10% of orders over $30)

CANADA S/H: $ ....
(20% of order)

TOTAL AMOUNT ENCLOSED: $_____

CANADA: CHEREV CANADA, INC. 1(800) 263-2408 FAX (519) 986-3103 · ENGLAND/EUROPE: WINDRUSH PRESS LTD. 0608 652012/652025 FAX 0608 652125
AUSTRALIA: GEMCRAFT BOOKS (03)888-0111 FAX (03)888-0044 · SPECTRUM ACCESS (617)357-1555 FAX (617)357-1771 · NEW ZEALAND: PEACEFUL LIVING PUB. (07)571-8105 FAX (07)571-8513